the **groom's** instruction manual

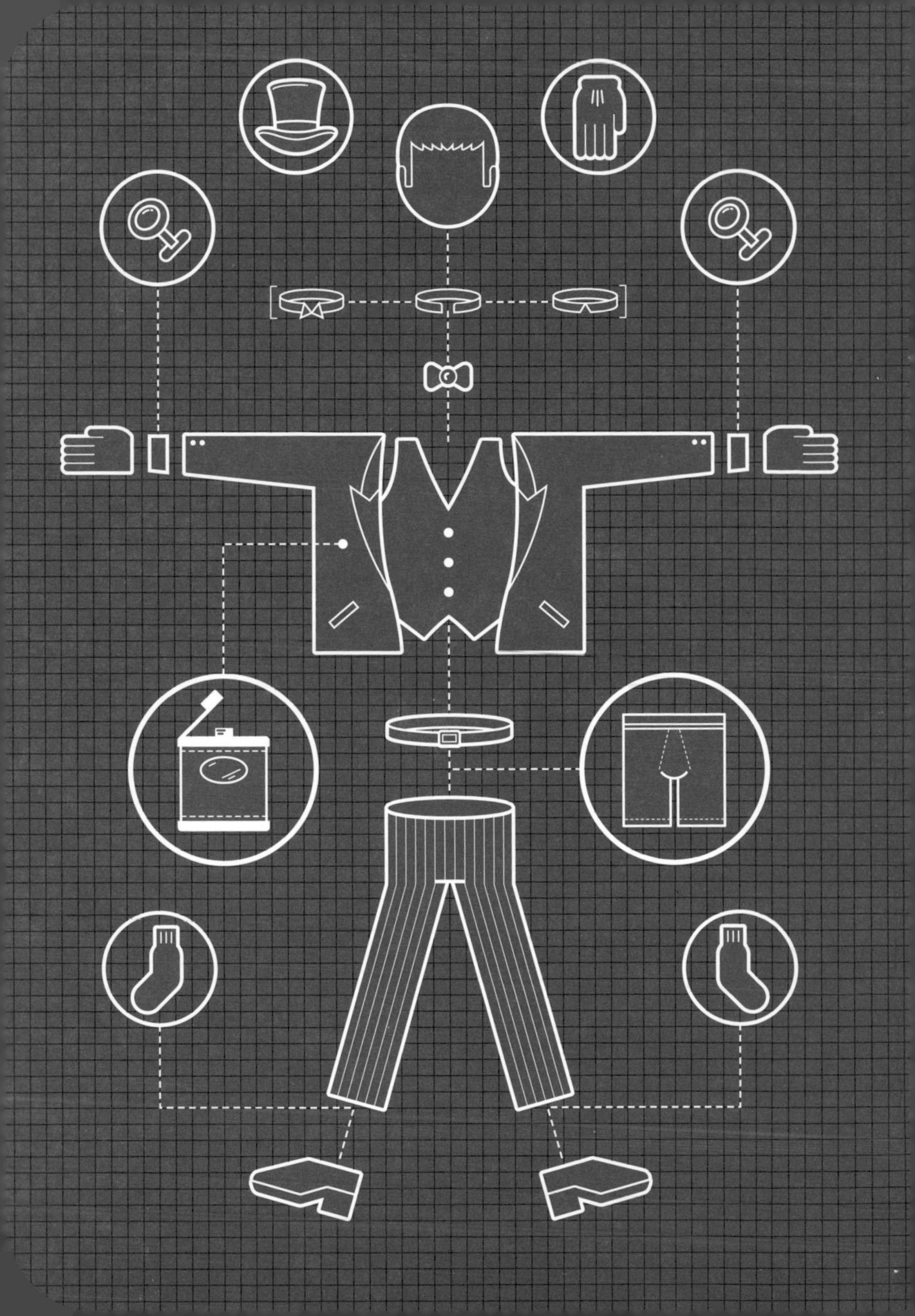

the

groom's instruction manual

HOW TO SURVIVE AND POSSIBLY EVEN ENJOY THE MOST BEWILDERING CEREMONY KNOWN TO MAN

by Shandon Fowler

Illustrated by Paul Kepple and Jude Buffum

QUIRK BOOKS
PHILADELPHIA

Library of Congress Cataloging in Publication Number: 2007931469

ISBN: 978-1-59474-190-6

Printed in China
Typeset in Swiss

Designed by Paul Kepple and Jude Buffum @ Headcase Design
www.headcasedesign.com

Production management by Chris Veneziale

10 9

Quirk Books
215 Church Street
Philadelphia, PA 19106
www.quirkbooks.com

Contents

Congratulations!

ATTENTION!

If you're reading this book, you must be head-over-heels in love with your fiancée! You're ready to take the plunge and get married! You're gonna spend hours drafting a seating chart for all of your guests! You can't wait to interview florists! And photographers and caterers! And musicians and clergymen and wedding planners! Your wedding is going to be The Greatest Day of Your Life and you are totally, totally stoked!

Or maybe—just maybe—you're a little bit scared.

If you fall into the former category, we salute you. (We're also incredibly freaked out by your enthusiasm, but that's another matter.)

If you fall into the latter category, we are happy to offer these words of comfort: It's okay to be afraid. Marriage is a big commitment, one of the biggest decisions you'll make in your whole life. Planning a wedding can often resemble a cruel fraternity hazing—you'll perform a series of ridiculous, frustrating, and often humiliating tasks just to prove you're worthy of standing before the altar.

Thankfully, your fiancée has plenty of advice at her disposal—hundreds and hundreds of books and magazines with frilly fonts and white covers and embossed gold foil. But today's multibillion-dollar wedding industry doesn't offer much in the way of guidance to men, despite that guys play a more active role than ever in the planning of their ceremonies and receptions.

A quick trip to the bookstore reveals two different types of resources for would-be grooms. The first consists of advice from a woman, a.k.a. a person who has never actually been a groom, or shopped for a tuxedo, or bribed the Tijuana police at a bachelor party turned sour. With all due respect to the fairer sex, this is advice you do not need. The second type comes from men who take their role in the battle of the sexes a little too seriously. Their primary concerns appear to be planning that wild bachelor party in Tijuana and negotiating an indestructible prenup.

We trust you want more from your groom's guide. Heck, you deserve more. You're a stand-up twenty-first-century gentleman. You're très moderne. You watch football and basketball, but you can tolerate an occasional romantic comedy, especially if Vince Vaughn is playing the lead. You'll thumb through *Playboy* and *Maxim*, but you really do read the articles (really). You are not a caveman. You want the wedding to have style and panache. You want your fiancée to be happy. You want your friends to look back on The Big Day with fond memories for years and years to come. "You crazy bastard," they'll sigh, shaking their heads in admiration, wishing they could travel back in time to relive your wedding all over again. "That was one hell of a night."

The Groom's Instruction Manual will walk you through every step of the engagement process—from crafting a perfect proposal (in case you still haven't done so) to drafting those thank-you notes after the honeymoon. You will learn what to wear and how to save on wearing it. You'll learn how to buy the perfect rings (yes, there will be more than one ring to purchase) for less. You'll get tips for picking a pro photographer, obtaining a marriage license, dealing with embarrassing relatives, and much, much more.

We'll also help you understand the psychology of your fiancée, her parents, your parents, and other major players in the wedding. There will be conflict ahead. Best to anticipate it now. Planning a wedding can bring out the worst in people. But to paraphrase James Taylor: When your fiancée is wigging out, your budget is imploding, your future father-in-law is threatening you with a monkey wrench, and your mother is in hysterics, just call out your *Instruction Manual*'s name, and you've got a friend.

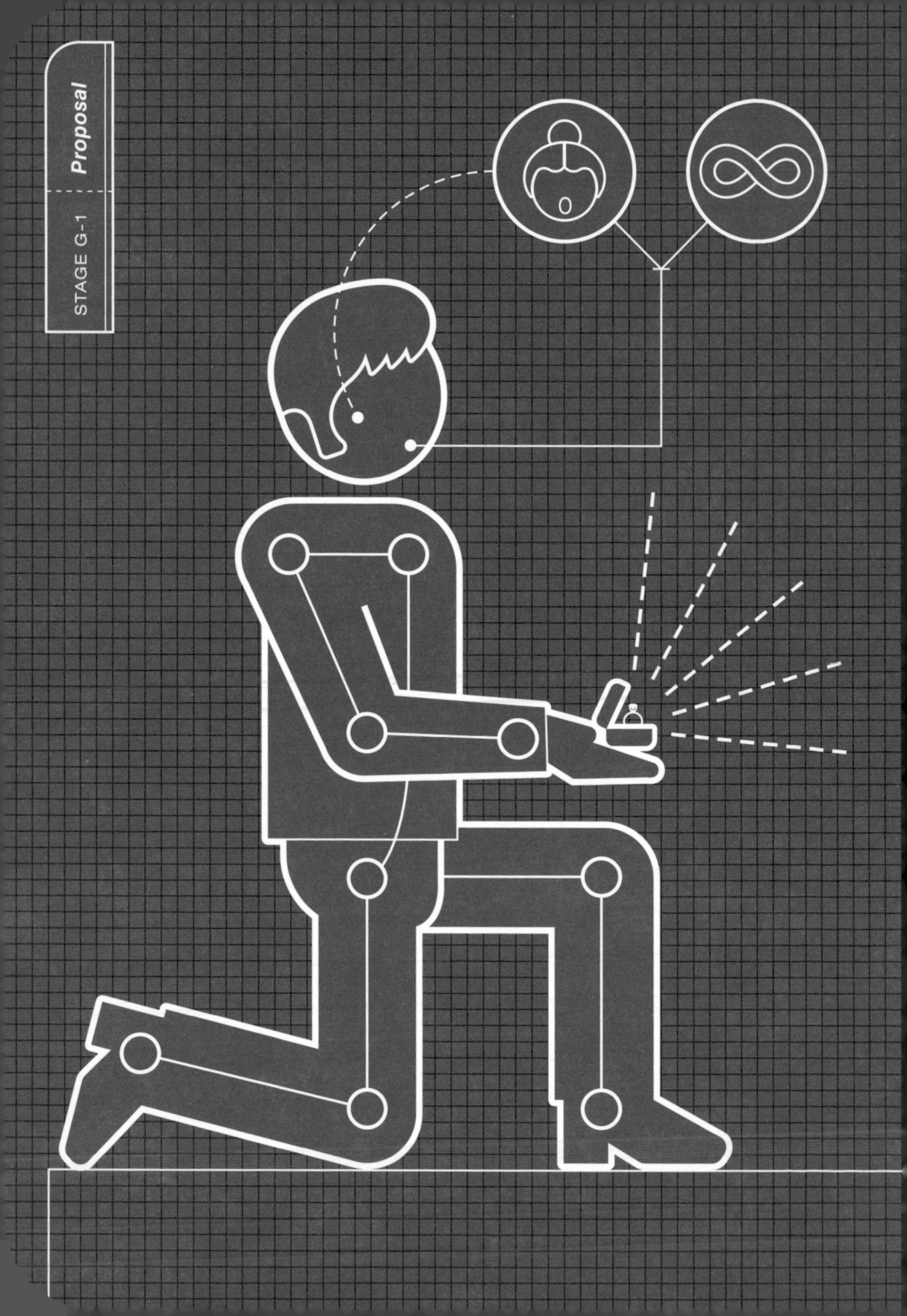

STAGE G-1
Proposal

[Chapter 1]

How to Get Engaged

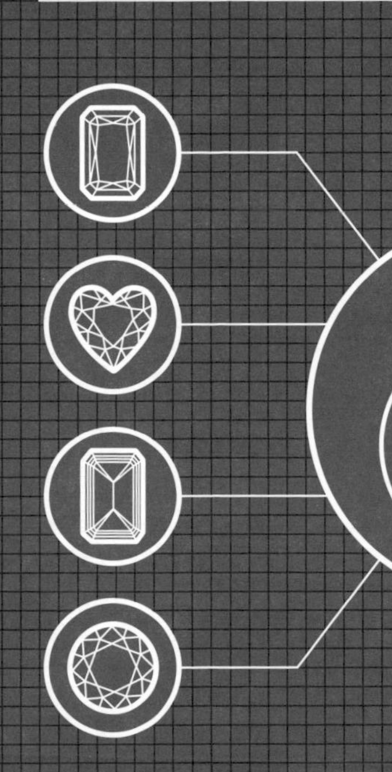

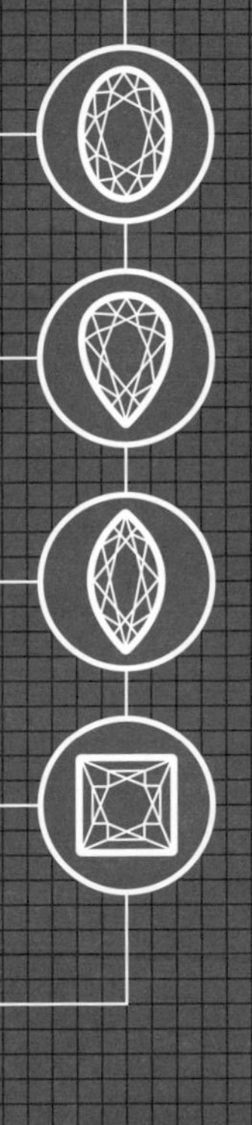

Confucius once said, "A journey of a thousand miles begins with a single step." This ancient wisdom can be applied to planning a wedding in the twenty-first century. Your journey will certainly feel like a thousand miles, and it will begin with a single step—asking the question "Will you marry me?" Hidden behind these four words are, well, quite possibly the rest of your life. Before you embark on this incredible adventure, let's take a few minutes to make sure you're ready.

Getting Married: A Pre-Screening

There are classes and workshops for virtually everything in life, and marriage is no exception. None of these classes is mandatory, however, and you are likely (and hopefully) going into this engagement with no firsthand experience as a married man.

Before you pop the big question and make a commitment that will endure the rest of your life, take this marriage pre-screening quiz and see how you fare on the road to engagement:

■ **Have you gotten the go-ahead?** ❑YES ❑NO

For most, this question is a no-brainer. We expect that you and your girlfriend keep open lines of communication and that not only have you talked about the future, you've talked specifically about your future together. But if that's not the case, you may be in for a rude awakening.

Let this question provide your first lesson: Always consider your mate's feelings—before the engagement, during the engagement, and forevermore. You will misread her feelings plenty, and she'll do the same to you, but if you're not copacetic on this first question, the time or the match is likely not right.

■ **Is your decision being made under duress?** ❑YES ❑NO

Perhaps you have trouble with commitment. Perhaps you've received an ultimatum from your girlfriend. Perhaps your mother, father, or potential in-laws are dropping not-so-subtle hints that you need to speed things along. Whatever the circumstances, you are the only one who can decide whether you're ready—so don't rush it. There's always counseling if you're just an indecisive wreck, but your marriage will only ever be as strong as your commitment to it.

■ **Is her decision being made under duress?** ❑YES ❑NO

A surefire way to blow an engagement is to coerce your girlfriend into making a decision. Even if you thought marriage was a foregone conclusion from your first date, you still need to let your potential wife make up her own mind in her own time.

■ **What was the name of your girlfriend's first pet?** ______________

Brace yourself: Engagement will bring out personality traits in your fiancée (and you) that you can't possibly expect or fathom. Before you get to that point, ask yourself how well you really know the woman you love. When did she graduate from high school? How many serious boyfriends has she had? Has she ever smoked? What's her mother's maiden name? What color are her eyes? These might seem like inconsequential details, but marriage is all about inconsequential details, so make sure you have the kind of relationship in which you share them with your potential spouse—and that you remember what's being shared—because you'll be spending a lot of time together. Which brings us to . . .

■ Do you understand the ramifications of what you're about to do? ❑YES ❑NO

To put it more bluntly, are you ready to spend the rest of your life having sex with the same woman—and only this woman—over and over again? It's surprising how many men don't understand that, in Western society, the most basic tenet of marriage is that you will be faithful to the same person, without reservation, for the rest of your life—or, depending on your religious persuasion, for all eternity. If, when it comes to matters of fidelity, you find yourself contemplating what the definition of "is" is, then perhaps you should consider a few more years of bachelorhood. And don't be fooled into believing your girlfriend if she's hinted that she'd forgive your future indiscretions. Few women will tolerate physical infidelity, and all of them demand and expect emotional fidelity.

■ Have you thought beyond the wedding day? ❑YES ❑NO

Some couples focus so much time and energy on how cool it'll be to get married that they overlook what it'll be like to *be* married. In your rush to throw the perfect party for friends and family, don't forget to consider what happens when the guests go home.

■ Have you talked about the things you're not supposed to talk about? ❑YES ❑NO

The old adage states: "Never talk about politics or religion in polite company." Fortunately, marriages aren't polite company. Democrats and Republicans, Catholics and Jews, Libertarians and Baptists have all made fantastic married couples. But before you get too far along, make sure that, no matter what your differences, you respect your partner's views and she respects yours.

■ Where do you stand on progeny? ❑0 ❑1 ❑2 ❑3 ❑4+

This question will be either the easiest or the hardest to answer. Either you both agree that you'll have the obligatory 2.4 children and a white picket fence within which said children will play and laugh and sing, or you will forgo merging your DNA to spend more time in Las Vegas and South Beach. But don't be surprised if your spouse's opinions on motherhood change after a dozen or so fruitless sojourns to the slot machine. You likely won't fare well with her change of heart by simply restating the terms of your verbal contract, so it's best to go into marriage with this assumption: Even if she says she never wants children, you'd have 'em with her anyway.

■ If you're having kids, who/what will they worship? ________
Where? __________ What denomination? ________________

You should also get a sense of how you'll raise children if you plan to have them. Will they go to Hebrew School, Sunday School, or the bowling alley? Will they say "yes, sir" and "no, ma'am" or "please" and "thank you"? Will they root for the Yankees or the Mets? And how many of them will be doing the rooting? You shouldn't expect to map out your whole life before you even buy a ring, but you should have a sense of what it'll mean to the two of you to wear your rings.

■ **Does your area code matter?** ❑YES ❑NO

If you're both from the same hometown, you're living there now, and you couldn't think of a better place to settle down, then skip this question. If you met anywhere but your or her hometown, talk about where you want to end up. Hopefully you can live anywhere as long as the woman you love is with you. But you should still make sure that "anywhere" really means anywhere, and you should make sure your fiancée-to-be sees things the same way. If this matter is going to cause a serious conflict, you're probably already feeling it deep in your gut, and you'll want to resolve it before things get too far along.

■ **Do you have reasonable expectations of your girlfriend?** ❑YES ❑NO

■ **Does she have reasonable expectations of you?** ❑YES ❑NO

Psychological opposites can make for some of the most harmonious and fruitful couples when your expectations of one another are clear and explicit. However, if your wife expects that after marriage you will become a rock-steady C.P.A. like her dad and leave behind the artsy "freelancer" life you inherited from your mom, or vice versa, it's best to know that—and accept it if you like—before signing a long-term contract.

■ Do your friends like your girlfriend? ❑YES ❑NO

Some will say that it should never matter what your friends think of the woman you love. Others say "bros before hos." Regardless of your opinion, your friends are what's called a "tell" in poker: They reveal much about you that you might not realize. Their opinions certainly will be their own, but in them you might find some truths about your own relationship with your girlfriend and with your friends as well. The point of this question is not to set you off on an anxiety-ridden soul-searching in which you use your friends as a litmus test for your girlfriend, but rather to determine where everyone will fit once you advance to the next level in your life. If there's no friction, fantastic. If there is, try to figure out the cause because the more you can figure out before you pop the question, the more you can avoid confrontations with friends and/or your fiancée down the road. Finally . . .

■ Do *you* like your girlfriend? ❑YES ❑NO

It sounds like an incredibly cruel and pessimistic question, but it also serves an important purpose. There is such a thing as love without friendship. It may be that you and your girlfriend make the perfect couple at a cocktail party. But are you just as happy with her when you're stuck at home and the cable isn't working? Hopefully you know all the small details about her life (see above) because you cherish her company and want to know everything about her. But if not, you may want to think harder about what will make you truly happy in a relationship.

Engagement Rings 101

Asking a woman to marry you without a ring is like asking a mattress salesman to seal the deal without the free pillow—they'll do it, but many won't feel right about it. True, a few men will be seized by a moment, throw caution to the wind, and pop the question on the spot. If that happens to you, we hope the woman you love will not let the absence of a ring prevent her from saying yes. But don't think that all your passionate spontaneity will get you out of eventually buying some hardware.

Finding an engagement ring is a mystery wrapped in a riddle shrouded in an enigma, and it may prepare you ever so slightly for what's in store for you as an engaged (and, soon enough, married) man.

Your goal is to find an everlasting symbol of your love, something that your wife will wear every day for the rest your lives together. If the woman you love isn't prone to buying anything she wants to wear three months—let alone fifty years—from now, then you understand the challenges you will face. Here are some general rules to help you make your decision.

Study like it's finals week. Jewelers exist because of romance. Romance can and will prevent us from thinking straight. Jewelers can and will take advantage. There are plenty of reliable Web sites that will illuminate you on the dos and don'ts of shopping for precious stones. Use them, because even if you have the best jeweler in the world, you're better off understanding stone ratings, carat weight, and other concepts before someone offers to teach you while you're holding their jewels in your hands.

Know the Four Cs. If you're not the studious kind, you should at a bare minimum know the Four Cs, which you'll hear just about anywhere you go. So, ba-ba-ba-bum, here they are:

Color: If you've seen the movie *Beautiful Girls*, you'll remember that Michael Rapaport's character bought his estranged girlfriend an engagement ring that he claimed was champagne-colored but everyone else recognized as brown. Likewise, if you're looking at diamonds that are not standard "blue" (really clear) and you notice that they're a lot cheaper, it's because they're not considered as good. Your girlfriend is almost certainly aware of this fact, by the way.

Cut: This term refers to the general way the diamond is "cut" into shape but not the shape itself. Cut affects how light travels within a diamond and influences the brilliance (or sparkly nature) of the stone.

Carat Weight: Just like buying ground hamburger or trail mix, what impacts the cost of diamonds the most is the weight. A stone that weighs three carats is generally half as heavy as (and at least half the price of) a stone that weighs six carats. Of course, you probably won't be buying a three-carat or a six-carat diamond, unless your wedding is being underwritten by a reality TV show with an insanely high budget.

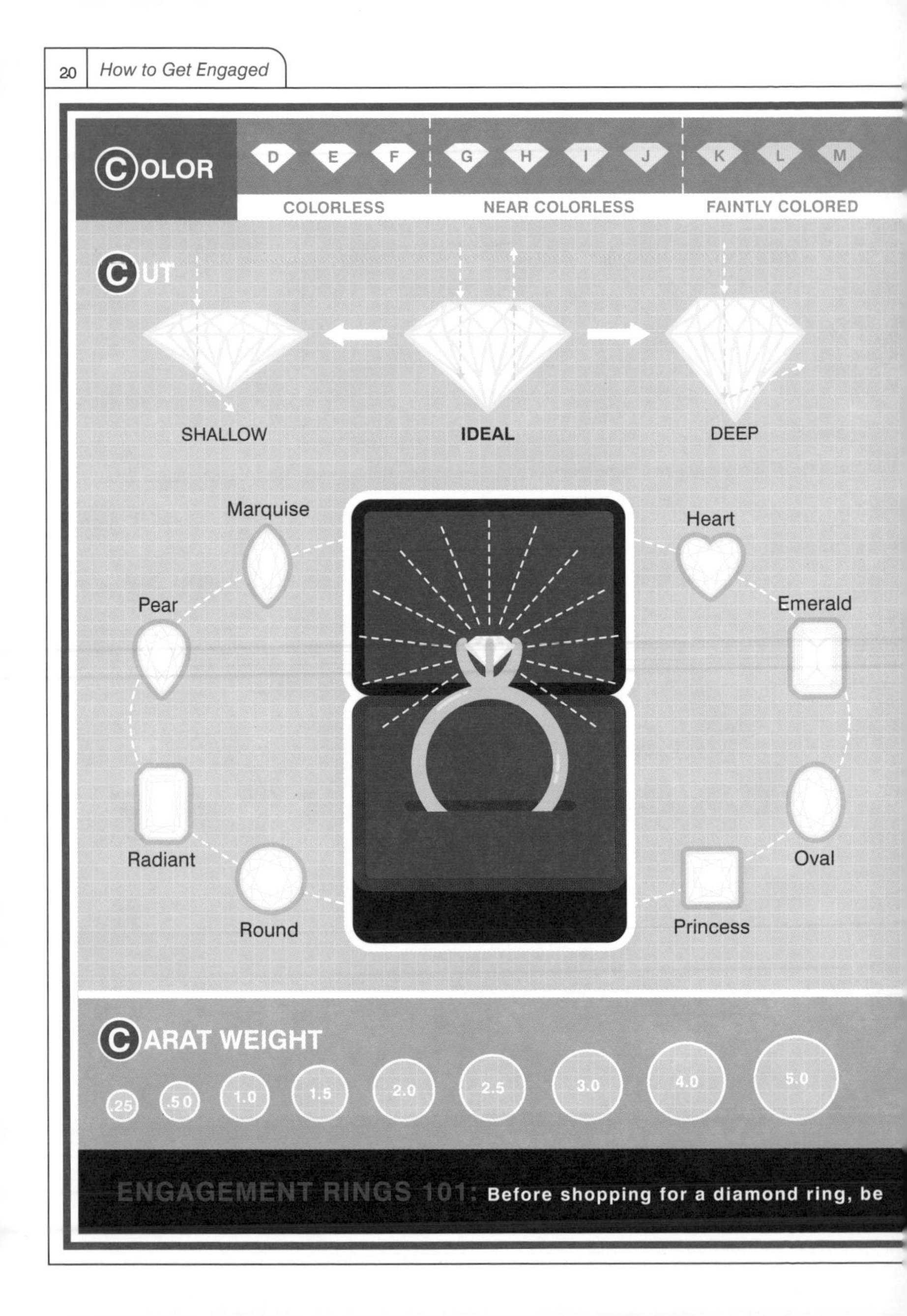
COLOR
D
E
F
G
H
I
J
K
L
M
COLORLESS
NEAR COLORLESS
FAINTLY COLORED
CUT
SHALLOW
IDEAL
DEEP
Marquise
Heart
Pear
Emerald
Radiant
Oval
Round
Princess
CARAT WEIGHT
.25
.50
1.0
1.5
2.0
2.5
3.0
4.0
5.0
ENGAGEMENT RINGS 101: Before shopping for a diamond ring, be

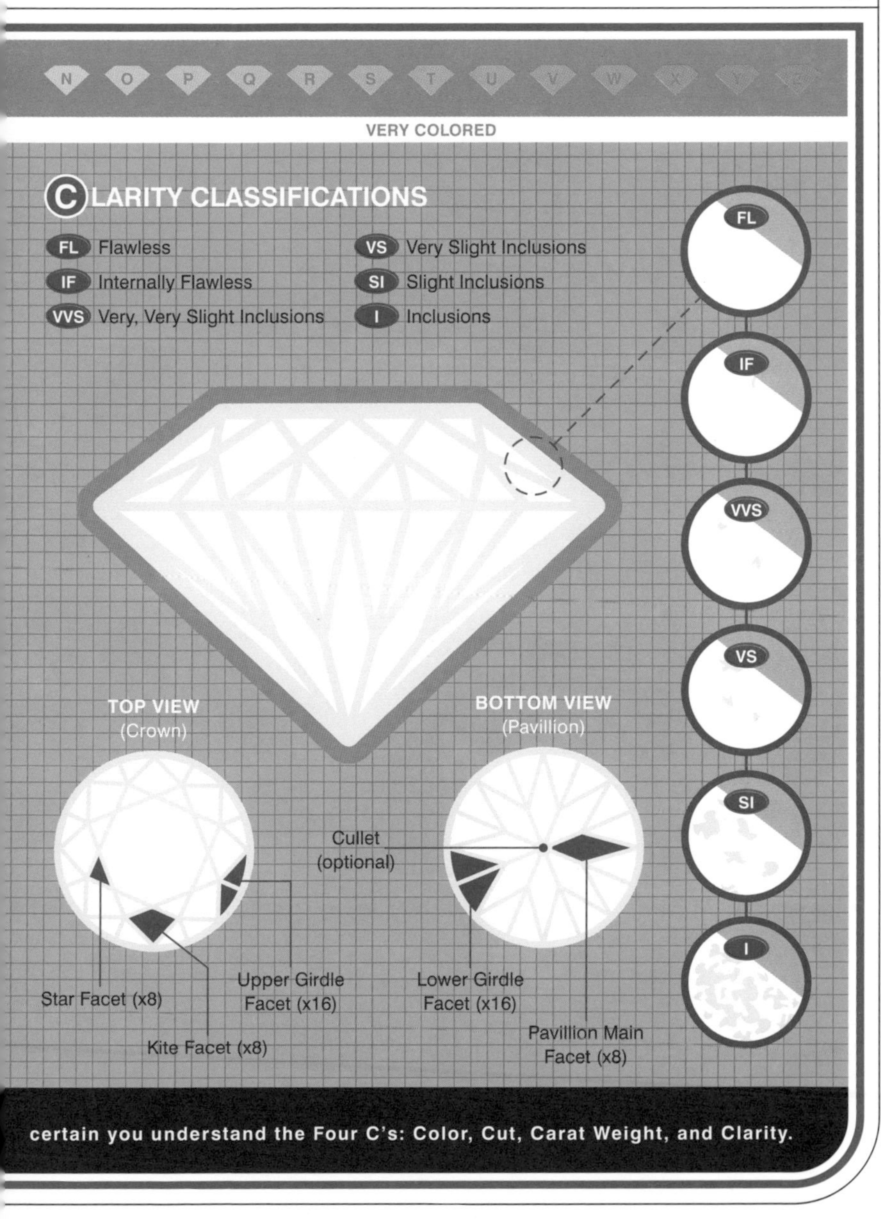

certain you understand the Four C's: Color, Cut, Carat Weight, and Clarity.

If you're looking to provide maximum bang for your buck, consider that two smaller diamonds weighing a combined 1.5 carats will look larger together in a setting than a single 1.5-carat diamond, and they may be slightly less expensive.

⚠ ***CAUTION:*** *"Carat weight" should not be confused with "karat," which in the United States is a measure of a metal's purity. Twelve-karat gold is 50 percent pure; twenty-four karat gold is 99.9 percent pure—as good as it gets.*

Clarity: Another major factor in determining cost is the clarity, or "flawlessness," of a stone. Any imperfection in a diamond is called an "inclusion," which could be anything from an air bubble that slightly clouds its luster to a slight nick made during the cutting process. As you look at stones and/or rings, you'll see such classifications as FL-IF ("Flawless" or "Internally Flawless," the highest quality), VVS (Very, Very Slight Inclusions), VS (Very Slight Inclusions), SI (Slight Inclusions), Inclusions, Spotted, Heavily Spotted, and Rejected.

You probably won't be able to tell the difference between most diamonds above the VS categorization without an extremely careful examination. But, then again, your fiancée (and her girlfriends, and her family, and her officemates) will be examining the ring extremely carefully. Few status symbols are as inexplicable as diamond rings, so balance carat weight with quality when your budget permits.

You'll notice that "cost" is not one of the Cs. That's because you should take one of two approaches to finding a ring. Either determine up front what you can pay and factor in the four Cs accordingly, or throw financial responsibility to the wind and go for broke. Either way, it helps to become a semi-expert on the subject.

⚠ ***CAUTION:*** *As both a status symbol and an item upon which most people are not experts, a diamond must be certified so that you know you're not being duped. These certifications are given at the original point of sale (frequently a diamond market in Europe), and once you see a couple of them you'll know what you should be looking for to make sure your diamond is legit.*

Go Covert. More important than knowing your product is knowing your customer. You can learn a lot about your girlfriend's tastes by simply paying attention (this theme recurs throughout this manual, so get used to it). Does she wear rings and other jewelry? If so, what do they look like? Is she all about the bling or is she a classicist? If you're not sure, go through her dresser drawers (just use common sense and wait until she's left the house). By looking at the jewelry she already owns, you can get a great sense of her style without tipping her off. Plus, if you're really stealthy, you can borrow one of her rings for a jeweler to measure, ensuring that the engagement ring will be a perfect fit. Just make sure you get it back before she notices that anything is missing.

Avoid trends. Getting a Tiffany engagement ring may feel like turning your soul (and life savings) over to The Man, but there are reasons those plain diamond settings have been popular for more than a century—great quality and simple design. You may think "plain" is passé, but consider how a diamond-encrusted band that spells "MY SHORTY" will look on your shorty's finger when she's sixty-five. *That* said . . .

Avoid proxy buying. Just because Tiffany sells lots of engagement rings doesn't mean the woman you love wants or needs one. Jewelry is notoriously priced for its intangibles (who designed it, the name of the jewelry store, where the jewelry store is located, etc.), so basically you can get the same ring for five different prices at five different stores. Shop around and get to know your options. That said . . .

Don't be a cheapskate. If your girlfriend has always dreamed of an antique Edwardian engagement ring, a cheaper imitation just won't do, even if she's the only one who can tell the difference. A good rule of thumb you'll find written many places, including right here, is that your engagement ring should cost you two-months' gross salary. That may seem like a lot, but this purchase is unlike nearly any other you'll ever make. Clothes, cars, electronics, even houses will all come and go, but there's some truth to the ad line "diamonds are forever."

Give yourself a time cushion. Rings aren't DVD players; even though you'll see dozens or hundreds in a showroom, it's unlikely you can point to a ring and bring it home the same day. Depending on your jeweler, you may have to wait anywhere from one week to several months before you actually have ring in hand. So start looking yesterday.

Keep it in the family. If you want to be a sentimental hero *and* a smart shopper, give your girlfriend a family heirloom. Maybe her mother or your mother has been saving her own engagement ring, or her mother's ring, or her mother's mother's ring, for exactly this occasion. Ideally, this will be a ring she always admired growing up, and she'll melt when you slip it on her finger. Plus, your family and/or future in-laws probably won't charge you retail, so you stand to save a few bucks to put toward the wedding or honeymoon.

Identifying the Best Ring for Your Fiancée

Here you are, a young man blinded by love, overwhelmed by books, magazines, and TV commercials telling you that it's okay to blow four paychecks on something that, if you're flush, weighs a few ounces. To make matters worse, you'll have to select this ring on the sly with minimal input from the person who will wear it. Fortunately, several strategies will help you identify the best ring for your girlfriend.

Listen to her. We cannot stress this point enough. The typical male mind conserves energy by listening only when prompted. Chances are that your girlfriend has expressed her opinions about jewelry on several occasions, even if you can't remember these conversations happening. So you'll be well served to keep your senses heightened from now on.

Talk around the issue. Psychologists recommend that we avoid, well, *avoiding.* But for the sake of finding the right ring, you should ixnay direct questions and find another way to bring up the subject without raising suspicion. If she wears other rings, throw her compliments with an eye toward getting her to say what she likes about them. Or get her into a jewelry store under false pretenses (go to have your watch repaired, buy your parents an anniversary gift, etc.). Once you're in the store, watch her reaction to different items. Or prompt her by pointing out rings you don't like; you're more likely to get an honest response and not draw suspicion by saying what you dislike, even if you're just pretending.

Enlist her friends and family. If your girlfriend has a sibling, mother, best friend, or somebody else you can trust not to spill the beans, enlisting this person to do reconnaissance work can be extremely rewarding. A sister can talk to your girlfriend about rings without raising suspicion. A mother or father might be able to give some family context. You don't want to get too many people involved because one of them might slip up and spoil the surprise—but one or two well-placed moles will make your task much easier.

Asking for Permission

You and your girlfriend will enter the engagement and the marriage as equals—that's a given. However, there's one tradition left over from more patriarchal times that may be expected of you

or may be worth performing even if it's not: speaking with your girlfriend's father and/or mother before popping the question.

As a matter of courtesy and ingratiation, reaching out to her parents can make them feel comfortable about your intentions with their daughter, and it conveys that you will consider yourself a part of her family's life as well as hers. You may not want to take the traditional route of asking her father for permission, as that might appear chauvinistic to your girlfriend—and you should try to get a sense of where she might stand on this. But informing one or both parents of your intentions before asking your girlfriend will, in most cases, increase your standing in her family's eyes as well as hers.

Setting the Stage

In love, as in retail, where you make your pitch can be as important as what you're pitching. Anyone who's been to a major sporting event is familiar with the JumboTron proposal: "Linda, I ♥ you. Will you marry me?—Bill." A collective "Awww" rises from the crowd as the cameras find Linda and Bill; under the gaze of 50,000 people, Linda processes what's happening, Bill alternates between looking into his girlfriend's soul and riling the crowd with some fist pumps, and the crowd holds their breath for the third act, which promises to be a moment of pure elation . . . or incomprehensible shame.

Luckily, things usually work out for the best, at least for the fifteen seconds that the Lindas and Bills of the world are on the big screen. What's more tenuous is what happens when the camera moves on to the wacky cowbell guy, and Linda, Bill, and the rest of section R, row 12 are left to process what just happened. Will Linda remember it as one of the greatest moments of her life? Or as "that time my ex-boyfriend proposed to me on the JumboTron"?

It is in nearly everyone's nature to gravitate toward comfortable, familiar settings. A lot of men like sporting events. Hence, JumboTron proposals. Far be it from us to assume that there are no women whose first choice for the most important question of their lives would be televised in front of thousands of face-painted, inebriated strangers. And far be it from you to assume that it is your girlfriend's first choice.

Here are some considerations for finding elation in location.

Find Your Happy Place

Scouting the perfect location may be less work than you think. Perhaps there's a site that holds special meaning for you and your girlfriend. Or maybe there's a spot that means a lot to you, and you'd like to share it with her. Before you go searching for a romantic setting that'll cost you a lot of money or may be crawling with other unimaginative romantics, search your own memory for the perfect place.

Decide Who Should Be There

Few questions are as personal and life altering as "Will you

marry me?" You'll want your girlfriend focused, whether you realize it or not. That could mean that it should be just you and her, but that's not strictly true. Having friends, family, or even strangers present can add fun, relieve the stress, and make the magic moment even more memorable. These are your options:

Friends: If your girlfriend is a social butterfly, it doesn't hurt to set the occasion in front of friends. This way, she shares the moment and basks in the glory, you are a romantic hero, and everyone can join the celebration. We suggest that you try to keep the event intimate, at least until the proposal. Just because friends are present and it's a momentous occasion doesn't mean you have to outdo every party you've ever attended. Speaking of which, stay sober. And make sure nobody else, especially your girlfriend, is drunk before you pop the question. It may seem like a no-brainer, but our hand-beer coordination flips into overdrive when we're nervous, so the sooner you take care of business, the more relaxed you can be.

Family: If your girlfriend is close with her family—and if you get along with them—a family gathering may be the perfect setting for a proposal. Just be sure she really, really wants to marry you, because there's nothing worse than being rejected in front of her mother, her father, your mother, your father, your brother, her sister . . . well you get the idea.

Just the two of you: No matter what the setting, your girlfriend may implicitly demand romance, and it's easiest to be romantic when you're alone. A romantic dinner at home, a romantic walk on the beach, a romantic sunset drive, a romantic weekend in the country—all these activities fit the bill. Another benefit of going it alone is that the moment can evolve more naturally into some celebratory consummation—but only if you're not saving yourself for the wedding night, naturally.

Public announcements: And thus we return to "The JumboTron Option." This kind of proposal has its benefits. You're almost guaranteed to surprise her. Plus, it could make both of you feel like temporary celebrities. But it can also be expensive (if you're paying for some kind of placement), logistically challenging, and far from foolproof. Before you proceed, consider the following:

■ **Make sure she would be into it.** If she constantly talks about that time she was on *Star Search* as a child, or she regularly calls in to the local morning radio show, or she made you stand outside in freezing rain to see *The Today Show* live, you're probably safe. If she makes not-so-flattering remarks about that kind of idiotic behavior from others, well, think about it . . .

■ **Make sure your plan is airtight.** With JumboTrons, morning-show proposals, TV ads, and the like, you have to make sure she is in fact watching for the five to fifteen seconds you'll be allotted. If she's not, you'll either have to explain what she just missed or cover up like you've never covered up before and figure out Plan B.

■ **Know when to take the public into private quarters.** Once you ask, you'll want to spend some one-on-one time with your girlfriend so you can enjoy a moment together—and immediately after she'll want to tell any friends or family who aren't there. That means the ballgame is pretty much shot. To make sure your first moments after engagement aren't too awkward, give her an out: Make sure she knows you're fine with finding some privacy, even if it's not halftime yet.

Co-opting Special Days

There are numerous benefits to popping the question on a birthday, anniversary, or holiday such as Christmas or New Year's. On the positive side, these events automatically bring families together in a festive setting—leaving you with much less planning to do. On the negative side, you may be unintentionally co-opting the occasion for years to come. Now, rather than just her birthday being about her, it will be about both of you. Rather than Christmas having all the traditions you know and love, it will also be about the start of your marriage. And in the unlikely event that your girlfriend rejects your proposal, you're bound to feel like she's killed Santa Claus—tainting a good holiday for many years to come.

Popping the Question

This is it—the moment of truth, ten or fifteen seconds that will change your life forever. With so much at stake, you may as well prepare yourself by reviewing a few pointers:

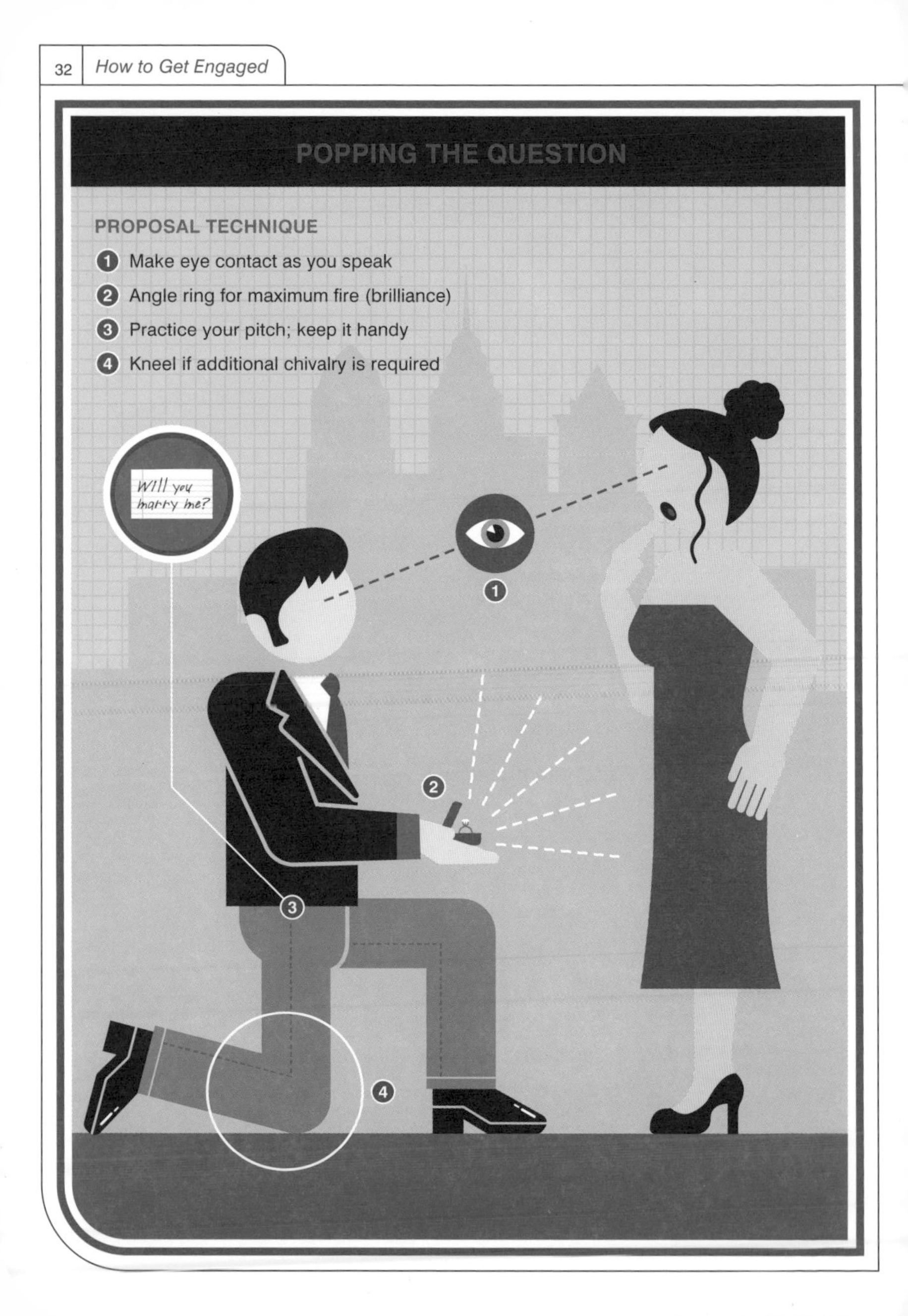
POPPING THE QUESTION
PROPOSAL TECHNIQUE
1 Make eye contact as you speak
2 Angle ring for maximum fire (brilliance)
3 Practice your pitch; keep it handy
4 Kneel if additional chivalry is required
Will you marry me?
1
2
3
4

To Knee or Not to Knee?

Kneeling during your proposal is old-fashioned and aristocratic to the core, but if your girlfriend dreams of a fairy-tale wedding, it's the best way to make her happy. If your girlfriend is easily embarrassed, on the other hand, you probably don't want to drop to one knee in a public setting, like a restaurant or an Aerosmith concert, because that is a surefire way to draw the attention of those around you.

Practice Makes Perfect

Most of us get flustered making speeches—and few speeches are as life-changing and nerve-wracking as a marriage proposal. You're putting your whole life on the line, so it's understandable if you want to bring a few notes on an index card. Better yet, practice what you want to say a few times until it sounds natural and unrehearsed, just like the proposals in movies.

Make Eye Contact

Remember, you're not asking her if she'd like fries or chips with her sandwich. When you ask this most important of important questions, make sure you are looking into her eyes and speaking clearly.

State Your Question in the Form of a Question

However you decide to ask her, make sure you're actually asking her. Yes, we know it's hard for you to leave yourself so emotionally bare. For that matter, we know it's hard to respect any book that uses phrases like "emotionally bare." But you need to suck it up. Don't couch your request in a self-protective nonquestion. ("You always said you wanted to get married, so I think we should.") Don't state what you want to happen in the situation. ("So, listen, I was thinking we should get married and then . . .") These are cowardly options, and you can do better. Remember, your girlfriend may have been waiting a long time for this moment, so you need to act like a gentleman and give her the option of saying yes or no.

If She Says No

There is the very real possibility that, despite your best efforts, your proposal will be declined. Depending on your demeanor, you might feel like sticking your head in the ground and never pulling it back out, making an unpleasant scene, or simply chalking it up as your girlfriend not knowing what she's missing. Any way you slice it, getting denied sucks. We're confident that if you're holding this book, you have a better-than-average shot at everything working out.

Just in case, here are several things ***not*** to do after your girlfriend says no:

- **Key her car with the engagement ring.** If you think being rejected sucks, try being the subject of a police report.

■ **Toss the engagement ring into a large, murky body of water.** You may have seen this done in movies, and in your current situation it has come back to you in a brooding flash. But remember that the thing that went over the bridge in the movie was a fake. Yours is real, and you really paid a lot for it.

■ **Exact revenge by sleeping with one or more of her friends.** That kind of behavior may be why she said no in the first place. Plus, if she rejected you, her friends might not be lining up to give you a go. Try sleeping with good-looking strangers—but do so responsibly.

■ **Call her mother or father to complain.** Life isn't a Jane Austen novel (thank heavens), so don't expect a call to her direct superior to be greeted openly and with a call to action on your behalf.

■ **Get drunk for the express purpose of telling her exactly how you feel.** Just don't go there.

■ **Tell her exactly how you feel while you're sober.** Okay, genius—if this is exactly how you feel, why'd you just ask her to marry you?

■ **Give up hope.** The world is full of stories of men who had to ask the woman of their dreams several times before she was ready to accept. Could be she's just not ready for the commitment, or it could be that she thinks you're not. Whatever the reason, don't give up hope the moment you hear no, because it could be more of a maybe.

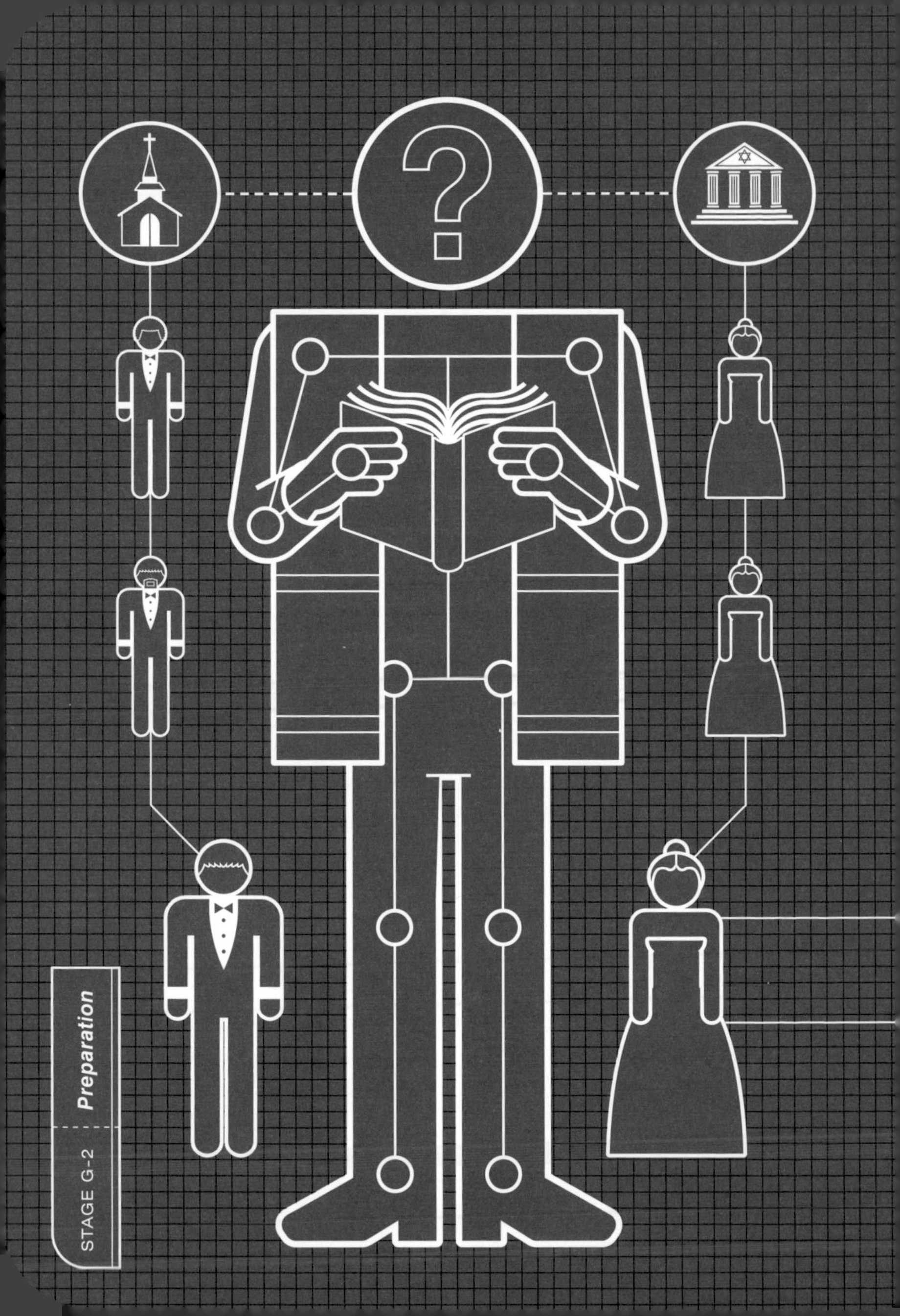
STAGE G-2
Preparation

[Chapter 2]

Getting to Know Your Wedding

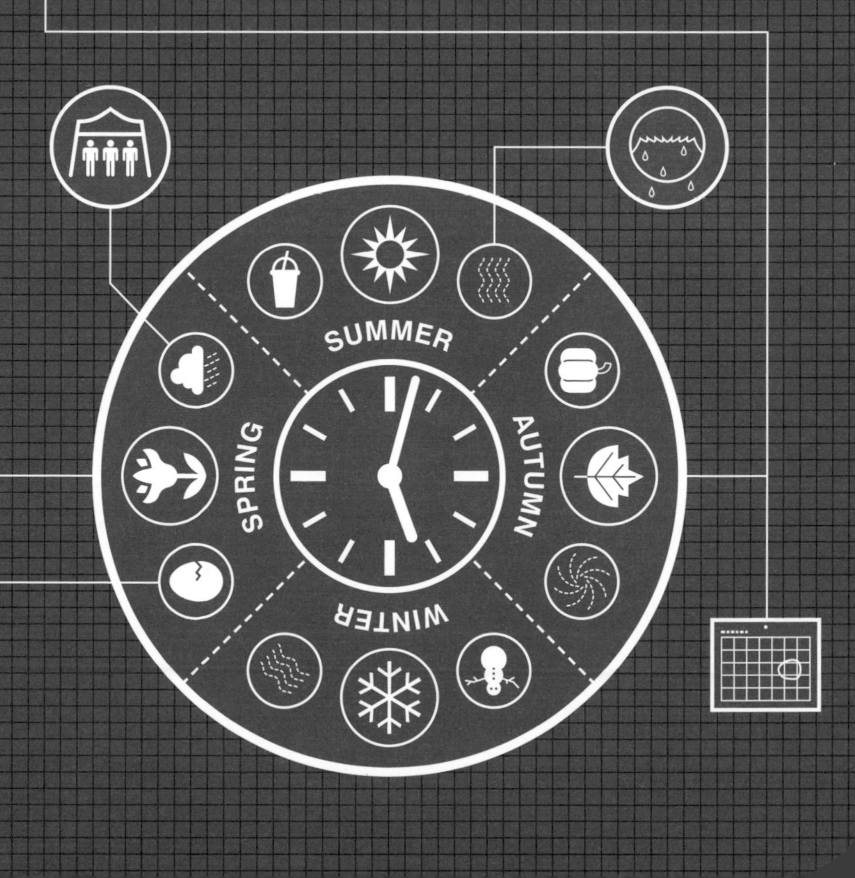

The euphoria you feel over your engagement will last approximately forty-eight hours. That's about the time it should take for everyone to wish you well and raise toasts in your honor. After that, the questions will start rolling in: Have you set a date? Where is the wedding? Have you picked your best man? Will there be an open bar?

You shouldn't let anyone, especially family members, rush you into any of these decisions. But you should consider them sooner rather than later. The more you plan, the less you (and your fiancée) will freak out.

Understanding Your Role in the Wedding

Up to this point in your matrimonial journey, you've been calling the shots. You bought the engagement ring. You planned the place and time for popping the question. You had a heart-to-heart with her father and/or mother. You made all the necessary arrangements with the JumboTron technician. In short, you've been in the driver's seat—but not for long.

You Are a Minority Stakeholder in the Wedding

Planning a wedding is a bit like starting a new company—albeit one with an outrageous marketing and refreshment budget and no chance of ever turning a profit. In this parlance, your fiancée is the majority stakeholder, especially if her family is covering the majority of the costs. That makes you a minority stakeholder, which means that your opinion will be heard, but you can't always expect it to matter.

Your Fiancée Is Always Right

Your engagement will be a time of many questions, and on all of them your fiancée will be right. Even when she's patently wrong, even when her aura has turned fiery red and reason has escaped her, even when the evidence is right in front of her that unequivocally proves her wrong, she will be right. Even when she has no opinion, when she is wracked with doubt, she will be right. She's right when she tells you that you can leave the wedding to her. And she'll be right when she tells you you're lazy and pathetic and you'd better start helping her out or else.

You'll likely approach this dilemma with mixed emotions. Perhaps you're a doer, a Type-A personality who is used to taking control and fixing things. Your fiancée is just being unreasonable, and you're ready to swoop in and help save her from herself.

Or maybe you couldn't care less about looking at flower arrangements, picking out wedding colors, and spending countless days poring over guest lists. You're more than willing to just go with whatever your fiancée suggests—if only she'd start suggesting things and stop asking for your opinion.

In either extreme and all points in between, you'll need to adjust

your expectations of what you know about the woman you love (more on this in "Distinguishing the Woman You Love from Your Fiancée," page 48) and make adjustments to your own behavior to account for your fiancée's changes. Fancy footwork has gotten you this far in the relationship, so don't let it fail you now.

The Engagement Checklist

Now that your expectations have been dialed down, here are few things you and your fianceé will want to consider:

When Should We Get Married?

Setting a date is the first step in any wedding planning because it grounds the event in reality, establishes a timeline, and allows participants and guests to make arrangements. The bottom line is that you can get married exactly when you want to; you just can't expect everyone to be available exactly when you need them. In addition, we suggest the following:

Defer to your fiancée's preference for the date. If she's always wanted a spring wedding, then spring it is. If she's more of an autumn type, set the date accordingly. If she has no preference, then weigh more heavily the considerations that follow.

Don't rush yourself. Most experts admonish that you need a minimum of six months to properly plan a wedding, and they're right. Granted, you can do all that's required in less time if you're supremely focused and your wedding plans are modest. But remember that you're not going it alone, and anyone you ask to be involved, or even just attend, will need ample planning time as well. Plus, sanity, like your fiancée, is something you might not fully appreciate until it's gone, so don't put more stress on yourself than is necessary. But . . .

Don't drag your feet. Some will say the length of the engagement doesn't matter because your premarital bond is strong and you were just "making it official." But trust us—you don't want to spend years talking about wedding preparations. Try to get everything wrapped up within six to fourteen months. If this feels too soon, go back to the Pre-Screening checklist (pages 12–17) and see if there's something you've missed. And if it's your fiancée who's dragging her feet, it's best to find out why sooner rather than later.

Consider family and friends. By no means should you pick your date based solely on what family members think. (If your fiancée's family is trying to dictate the wedding date, it can cause major consternation; if *your* family is trying to dictate the wedding date, it can lead to an international incident.) But if you want to have these people at your wedding, consider any obstacles that family and friends might face. Do military or similar obligations prevent someone from attending at certain times of year and/or certain locales? Do physical disabilities need to be taken into account? Are any of your friends planning a wedding around the same time? If you have the reception in a mountain meadow, will your oldest and youngest relatives be able to make the trek? Before you lock up a date, make a "must-be-there" list with your fiancée. Do your best to find a date that you both agree upon and that also works for as many of the "need-to-haves" as possible. Then find your Zen place knowing you took other people's availability into consideration.

How Big Should the Wedding Be?

As the majority stakeholder in the wedding—especially if, as tradition often dictates, her family will bear the brunt of the financial burden—your fiancée's opinion on the size of the wedding and most other issues should weigh twice as heavily as your own. And if her family is footing the bill, any disagreements based on cost can likely be maneuvered through them.

Perhaps you and your fiancée have already discussed the type of wedding you'll have. If so, you already have some understanding of what you're about to plan. But don't be surprised if her idea of the occasion has changed dramatically between when you talked about getting married and when you got engaged. Your fiancée is now operating under a different set of internal rules (see "Distinguishing the Woman You Love from Your Fiancée," page 48), and she may not take kindly to being held accountable for any past statements.

None of this is meant to assume that your fiancée will be unreasonable, because she's still the same person you asked to marry you. Just keep in mind that you're talking about matters far

more meaningful than where you should go for Sunday brunch. She's taking it seriously, and she'll be able to tell if you're doing the same.

How Much Can We Spend?

Ah, finances. Here is the area in which you won't be able to simply sit back and enjoy the ride. Your fiancée probably started planning her wedding years before the two of you met, and she isn't about to let a checkbook stand between her and her fairy tale.

Having the bride's family cover all wedding expenses is a somewhat chauvinistic tradition akin to a dowry, but it can also be a huge score. If you find a family with such traditional values, bless their hearts. More likely, however, the financing of your wedding will be a group effort: You will contribute, your fiancée will contribute, and (hopefully) both families will contribute. Try to get a sense up-front of how much you'll have to spend, and then stay actively involved in keeping track of your expenditures. You don't want to go bankrupt, but that shouldn't prevent you from thinking ambitiously. You're planning for a day that you want to remember fondly for the rest of your life—and, more important, that your fiancée wants to remember. So socking away more now will make for a happier bride and groom when the big day arrives.

On the flipside, you need to be firm and reasonable if your fiancée is not taking kindly to spending limitations. You can avoid telling her something can't be done simply because you can't afford it by thinking of appealing, and cheaper, alternatives. Better yet, if you can find a sympathetic ear among her parents, siblings, or close friends, talk to them about providing alternatives so that you don't have to be the bad guy.

Finally, whoever ends up contributing, make sure you do the gentlemanly thing and thank them.

Where Should We Say "I Do"?

Once the budget is resolved, you can go back to functioning like a minority stakeholder, which means that your opinion on the location of the wedding is largely irrelevant. Your fiancée may be leaning toward her hometown, a favorite vacation spot from her childhood, or any number of other places. Any objections you have should be considered carefully before you share them, especially if her parents are paying for the wedding. But even if they aren't, you will have to make a very convincing sentimental argument if you intend to get married at a favorite spot of yours.

Is God Invited?

Most wedding ceremonies occur in a church, synagogue, or other religious venue. And if they're not, they will still most likely be performed by somebody of a religious persuasion.

If you and your fiancée practice the same religion, no problem—though you may still have your families to consider if their beliefs do not match your own. In this case, you and your fiancée should be true to your own beliefs. It's your wedding, and if religion is important in your daily lives, you shouldn't let somebody else make your decision for you. And you certainly shouldn't let anyone coerce you into practicing traditions that make you uncomfortable.

If, on the other hand, you and your fiancée have not reconciled your religious beliefs, you are better off deferring to your fiancée. As important as it may be to you to get married as a faithful Presbyterian, you should understand and accept your wife's preference for a Lutheran ceremony. If your differences run deeper and your opinions are stronger, you should work them out before moving on. Your spirituality is something that you'll want to be comfortable about, especially if you're being asked to compromise it, even if it's just for an afternoon.

How Big Should the Wedding Party Be?

You may have always assumed that your dozen closest friends would be standing with you, whereas your fiancée planned on having only her sister by her side. Once again you should defer to the majority stakeholder, because your friends will get over it much sooner than she will. But, on the other hand, if she seems to want twice as many bridesmaids as you want groomsmen, definitely attempt a compromise. Just don't expect the compromise to go your way.

Engagement Checklist

Use this document to record the most basic para-
to your fiancée's wishes.

WEDDING CEREMONY

DATE __ __ / __ __ / __ __ TIME __ __ : __ __ ○ A.M. ○ P.M.

Location

Address (Number and Street) | City

State/Province | Country | Zip/Postal Code

WEDDING RECEPTION

DATE __ __ / __ __ / __ __ TIME __ __ : __ __ ○ A.M. ○ P.M.

Location

Address (Number and Street) | City

State/Province | Country | Zip/Postal Code

GUESTS __ __ __ x COST __ __ __ . __ __ = TOTAL __ __ __ __ __ . __ __

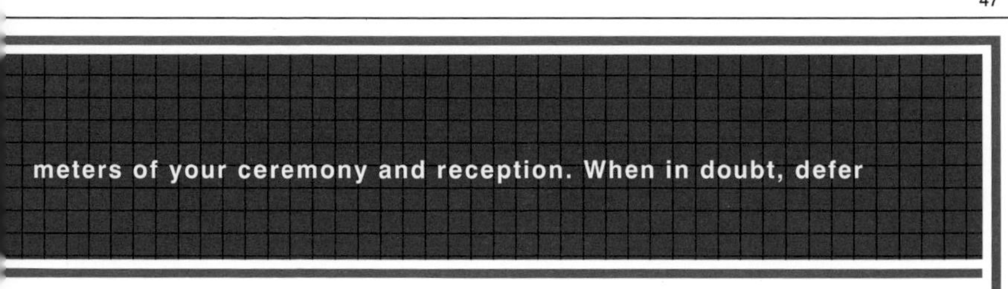
meters of your ceremony and reception. When in doubt, defer

RELIGION

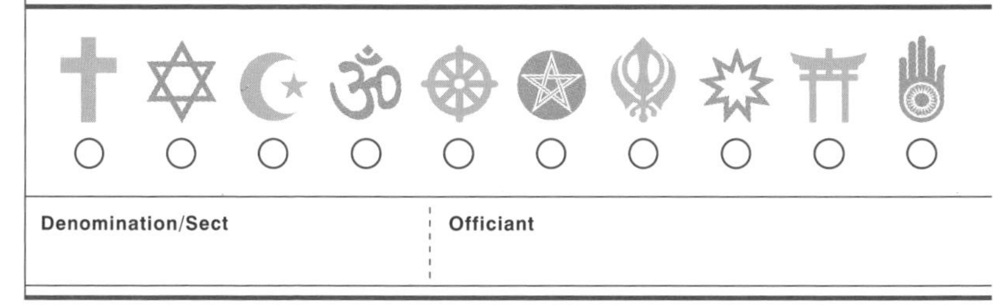

Denomination/Sect	Officiant

WEDDING PARTY

GROOMSMEN x ☐☐	Best Man	

BRIDESMAIDS x ☐☐	Maid of Honor	

What About Other Wedding Traditions?

Nearly all weddings come with an accompanying rehearsal dinner, which (if you follow the same traditions that oblige the bride's family to cover the cost of the wedding) is traditionally paid for by the groom's family. Other events surrounding the event will depend on religious considerations, family traditions, regions (everything you've heard about the extravagance of Southern weddings is true), and more. For the duration of your engagement, you will be a celebrity and will have many demands on your public-appearance schedule. Make sure to find out from your fiancée what to expect. Likewise, if the traditions lie on your side of the family, make sure your fiancée knows what's in store.

Distinguishing the Woman You Love from Your Fiancée

Before you delve even further into planning a wedding, take the time to familiarize yourself with the psychological transformation a woman may undergo and how that transformation will impact the tasks at hand.

The Woman You Love is easily recognized by several key traits:

- She means everything to you.
- She is beauty incarnate.

■ She makes you smile, comforts you, even makes Journey songs sound not quite so awful.
■ She gets along with your friends and family (mostly).
■ Should you choose to have children, she will be the perfect mother.
■ Most important, she is so indescribably special that you have asked her to be your wife.

Unfortunately, the Woman You Love often goes into hibernation for an indeterminate period between your proposal and the wedding, wherein your Fiancée takes over. You will recognize the coming of your Fiancée's blossoming through several telltale signs:

■ Increased agitation, bordering on or spilling over into aggression.
■ Decreased and/or sardonic shift in humor. It is not uncommon for humor to be displaced entirely by agitation or aggression.
■ The onset of a form of competitiveness that can be as fierce and inexplicable as the Cola Wars. Her singular drive is to outdo any wedding she's ever attended, watched on television, or read about.
■ Any mistake you make, regardless of severity, will be a black mark on your relationship-long record of ineptitude.
■ Simple and seemingly joyful tasks, such as taste testing wedding cakes, can bring her to tears or, possibly, blows.

Why Is This Happening?

Women undergo socialization in a much different manner than men. Whereas men can bond through something as simple as

watching a squirrel try to pick up a nut that's been glued to the sidewalk, women generally form bonds from sharing more emotionally significant moments: jobs and classes, relationships and breakups, cherished hobbies. As a result, women attach profound importance to social events, especially to those they host. In addition, men grow up pretending they're pro athletes, rock stars, and other generally irresponsible avocations. They likely never have imaginary tea parties or weddings. Hence, childhood fantasy merges with adulthood reality far more frequently for women than for men, turning even the most secular of ceremonies into a religious experience for your fiancée.

Her zealotry is only compounded by the mass media and popular culture. Our magazines and newspapers are plastered with photos of celebrity weddings; all romantic comedies, even if not strictly about weddings, usually involve a fairy-tale romance that ultimately leads to marriage; daytime TV talk shows sponsor "dream weddings" on a regular basis; and evening reality TV shows cover every excruciating moment of planning a ceremony. To influence the mind of a woman under such a pervasive spell is to confront a powerful force that you can't possibly comprehend—so don't bother.

What Has My Fiancée Done with the Woman I Love?

All this may appear to you as if the Woman You Love is speaking in tongues. But a reason does lie behind the transformation. Your

Fiancée, with her unquenchable thirst for perfection and cutthroat tactics, will plan a much better wedding than the Woman You Love because, as they say, great art comes from great hardship. Just don't forget that the Woman You Love is still in there somewhere, and that the more you help your Fiancée—by reassuring her when she needs reassurance and correcting her when she needs correction—the sooner you'll get back the Woman You Love.

The Players: A Personality Primer

As you embark on your engagement, numerous people will keep popping up, whether you like it or not. Requests will be made, and ultimatums will be presented. To avoid the latter and assure that the former run as smoothly as possible, you should familiarize yourself with the major players in your engagement and wedding.

Your Fiancée

Your Fiancée is a personality profile consciously or unconsciously adopted by the Woman You Love to ensure that she can achieve all challenges presented to her during the engagement (see also, "Distinguishing the Woman You Love from Your Fiancée," pages 48–49).

Physical Traits

■ **Beauty.** During the engagement, you may find that your fiancée appears more attractive than usual. This change may be a result of an increased emotional attachment brought on by the engagement. It will also frequently be brought on by your fiancée's intense wedding-preparation workout regimen. Either way, you are advised to offer compliments.

■ **Increased energy.** Your fiancée may be visibly energetic throughout the engagement, which may lead her to expect the same of you.

■ **Tight jaw, wide eyes.** This combination of physical traits could act as an early warning sign for one or several of the personality traits outlined below.

■ **Wide swings in appearance.** You may also find that, during engagement, your fiancée will dress up with more flair and dress down with more abandon. The former may be expected of you, whereas the latter will not and should be avoided whenever possible.

■ **Visible exhaustion.** You may also encounter redder, puffier eyes, unkempt hair, frequent frowns, and other signs that your fiancée could use more rest than she is getting.

Personality Traits

■ **Perfectionism.** Present in a majority of fiancées is a drive to make everything related to the wedding perfect. This perfectionism extends to all wedding-related tasks, regardless of size or comparative value, which can make her reaction to the management of your tasks unpredictable or predictably insatiable.

- **Mood swings.** While planning for the wedding, your fiancée may be affected in seemingly random ways by her numerous responsibilities. A moment of joy may be followed by anger or terror. A moment of anger may collapse into relief. Her emotional patterns can and will be unpredictable, making it nearly impossible to do away with them. But you can certainly be prepared for them.

- **Anxiety/uncertainty.** These emotions can be caused by other key players in the engagement, including you. Anxiety triggers include the expectations of family and friends, nerves related to the handling of the wedding by her and others, or thoughts about her commitment to the relationship.

- **Increased aggressiveness.** As stated in the previous section, the combination of perfectionism and uncertainty can lead your fiancée to become more prone to confrontation. Her aggression may be directed toward you, toward other key players in the wedding, or even toward innocent bystanders.

- **Exuberance.** Your fiancée may forgo many of the personality traits listed here and instead opt to see only the bright side of the engagement and planning. Every event will be a challenge to relish, as opposed to a burden to overcome. Every new day will present her with new tasks that she'll get, rather than have, to do immediately. Such circumstances are rare and should be enjoyed while they last.

Tools and Tactics

- **Don't tap the glass.** As in chess, the queen is truly the most powerful player on the board, and you, the king, are fairly powerless by comparison. Unlike the chess queen, the bride is also the most important player on the board. Everybody's there to protect her, including you, and even though you can move only one square at a time, you need to make those squares count. You shouldn't bend to her every whim, but a key to understanding how to keep her happy (thus keeping the engagement on track) is to provoke her only under emergency circumstances. In other words, most things you think are worth fighting for really aren't, at least not during the engagement.

- **Recaps are for *SportsCenter*.** We're happy to teach you about the physical and personality traits above, but the root of "tactic" is "tact," and we recommend you show some when attempting to counter one of your fiancée's newfound traits. In other words, saying something like "Honey, you're being unreasonable" will probably be taken as a call to arms rather than as a helpful pointer.

- **Deploy the compliment sedative.** If you are unaccustomed to paying your fiancée unsolicited compliments, the engagement is a good time to start. They can defuse a potentially volatile situation and/or turn an already-amorous moment into a sure thing. However, if you've already gone down a path of confrontation, compliments will only provide a distraction or, worse, act as fuel for your fiancée's anger or frustration.

- **Use the whole board.** Certain subjects will never be open for easy broaching between the future bride and groom. In such circumstances, remember that you are not alone. Maids-of-honor, bridesmaids, in-laws, and others can be recruited in getting a more satisfactory result than if you were to seek a result on your own.

- **Know your alpha.** Often your fiancée will require nothing more from you than your manly presence. She may just need to fold into your arms or let you make a final decision or confront a family member or friend. Whatever the reason, these situations should be considered your spotlight moments to prove that you can be the Alpha Male Protector. She may ask specifically for your manhood, but you should also learn when she is fishing for it.

- **Love your beta.** On the flipside, know when it's right to take charge and when you should be satisfied to make your one-square moves. You want to avoid being thought of as a chauvinist. Also, for obvious reasons of personal responsibility, you want to avoid shouldering the primary burden of wedding planning. So, even though it's okay to have opinions on the cake or the flowers, don't be surprised if the only person who cares about your opinions is the man in the mirror.

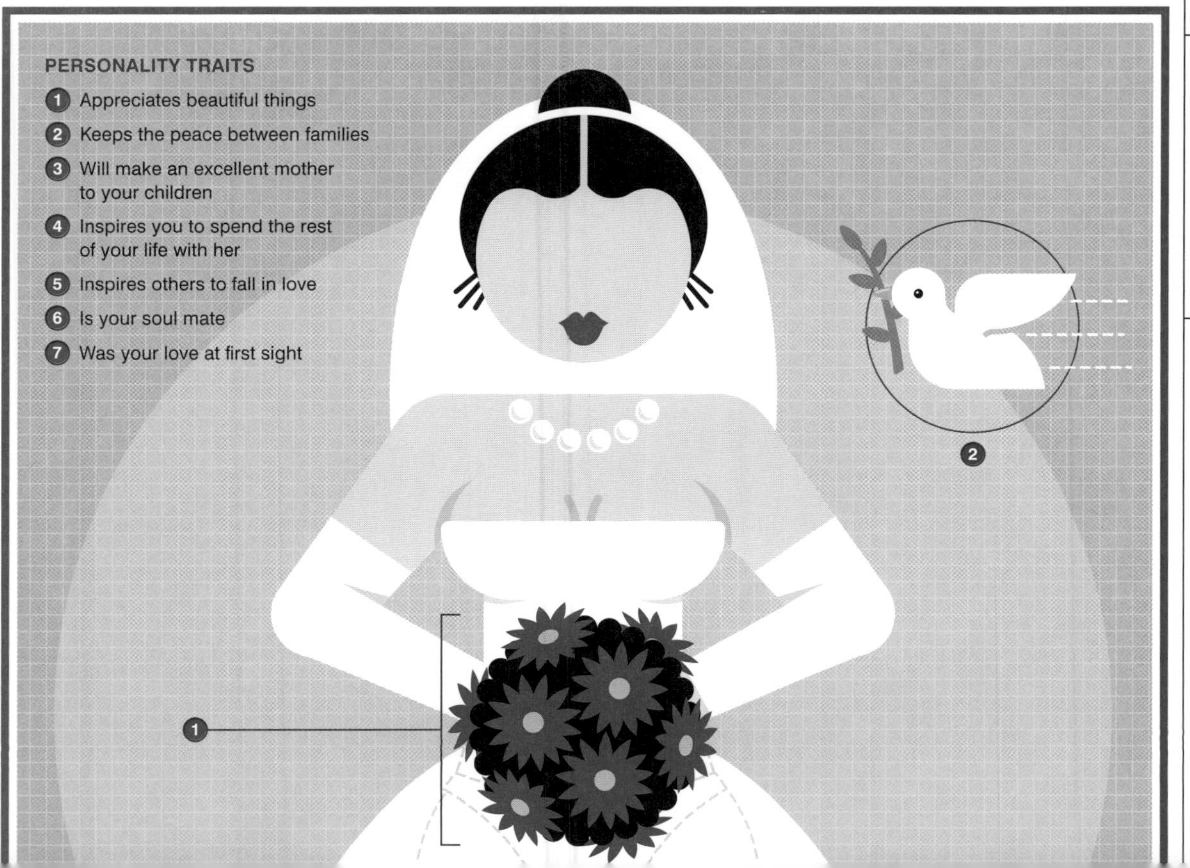
PERSONALITY TRAITS
1 Appreciates beautiful things
2 Keeps the peace between families
3 Will make an excellent mother to your children
4 Inspires you to spend the rest of your life with her
5 Inspires others to fall in love
6 Is your soul mate
7 Was your love at first sight
2
1

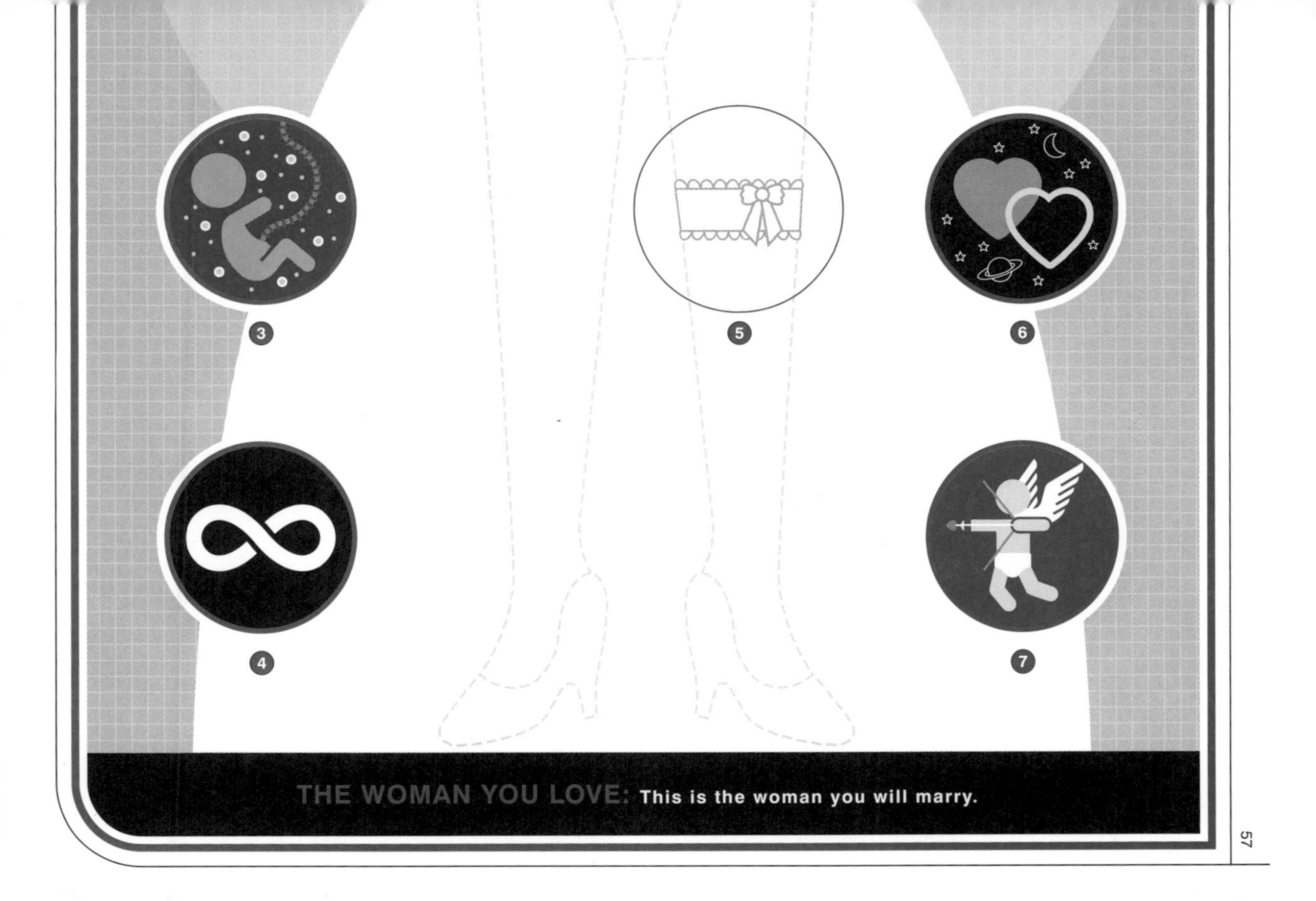
3
4
5
6
7
THE WOMAN YOU LOVE: This is the woman you will marry.

1
2
PERSONALITY TRAITS
1 Clenched jaw
2 Visible exhaustion
3 Mood swings
4 The most powerful player
5 Anxiety/uncertainty
6 Increased energy

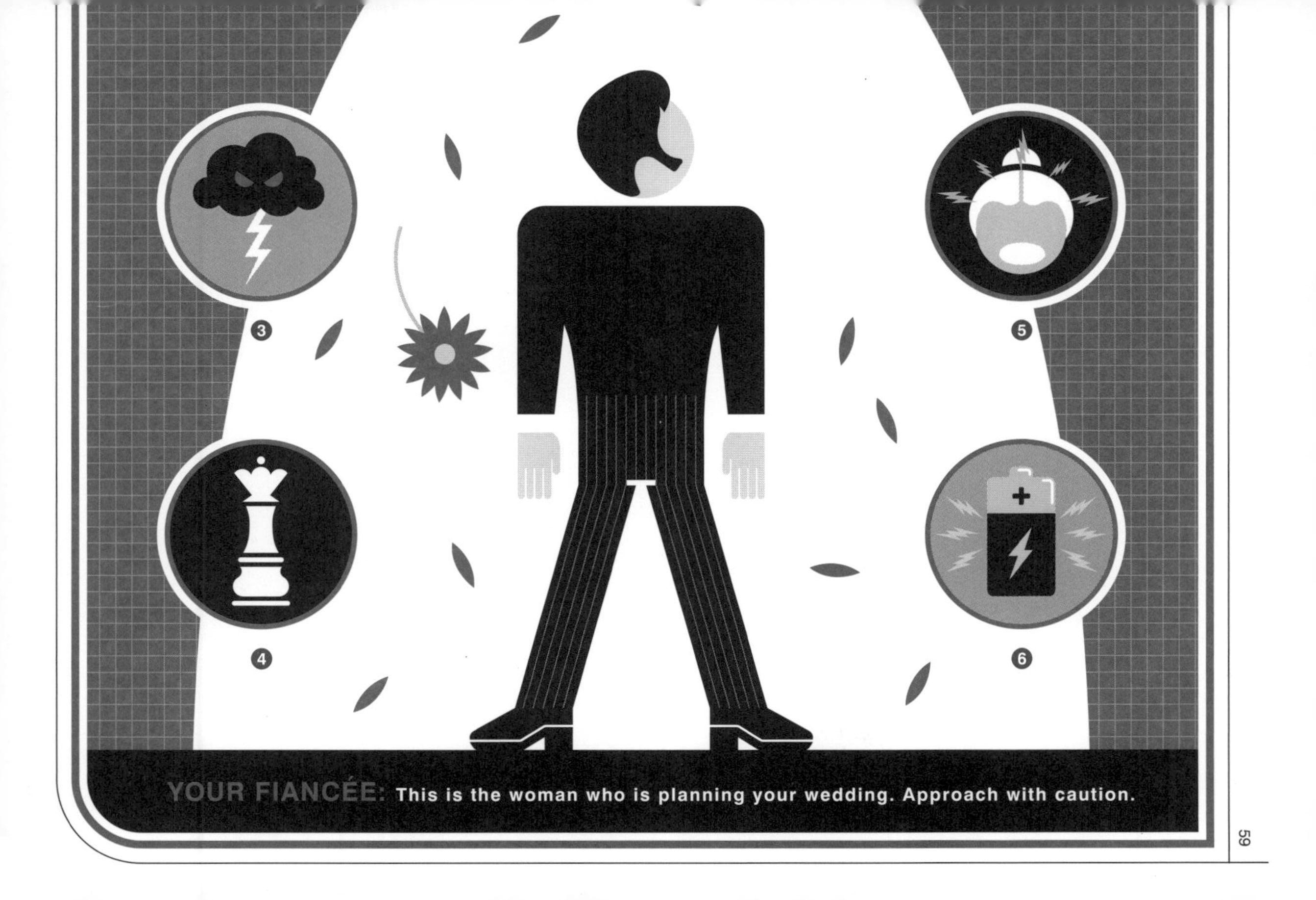

YOUR FIANCÉE: This is the woman who is planning your wedding. Approach with caution.

You

Hi. How's it going? You're the fiancé or, if you prefer, the groom. It may seem strange to read a definition of yourself, but you should understand what you'll be doing as the engagement proceeds. Let's start with chronology: You're listed second here to drive home the point that you are always the second-most important person in the wedding. Before you breathe a huge sigh of relief, keep in mind that being the second-most important isn't exactly stress free. In fact, over the course of the engagement, you may find yourself exhibiting a host of new personality traits.

Personality Traits

- **Mr. Romance.** There's nothing like an engagement to kick our romantic instincts into overdrive. You may find yourself experiencing a renewed desire to send flowers, go for walks in the park, write love letters, and all the other things you used to do in the early stages of courtship. These are all good instincts, and they will certainly pay dividends in the long (and hopefully short) run.

- **Mr. Headcase.** Weddings make even the calmest, most collected groom dissolve into a weeping shell of a man. Fortunately, being a fiancé means you get to designate others to be a temporary therapist. If you're feeling freaked out, let people know—anyone except your fiancée—before things are too far gone. And don't worry, you're not alone. Your married friends will tell you that they went through every emotion you're currently experiencing.

■ **Mr. Silent Partner.** You and your fiancée will make all sorts of decisions together, giving you a rare pre-marriage opportunity to prove that you're not a complete tool. Show a moderate amount of interest even when the subjects (bouquets, table settings) are the definition of uninteresting, and take charge when the situation warrants it. Your fiancée may not always see eye-to-eye with you, but she'll hopefully appreciate that you "care."

■ **Mr. Trophy Husband.** Throughout the engagement and especially on your wedding day, you will be paraded in front of a long line of friends and family you may have never met before. The litany of introductions may be overwhelming, and, combined with the expectations your fiancée levels at you when she's making them, you might feel like sabotaging every "hello" so that you can get the hell out of there. Fight the urge. Not only will a bad first impression linger for years, but you might also blow your shot at some pretty sweet wedding presents. You'll do well to maintain your gentlemanliness throughout the engagement, even if your cheeks start to hurt from all the smiling.

■ **Mr. Groom.** Finally, whatever tumultuousness you experience with your fiancée, put everything behind you on your wedding day. You will remember the day for the rest of your life, as will your bride. Make sure it's a memory worth keeping.

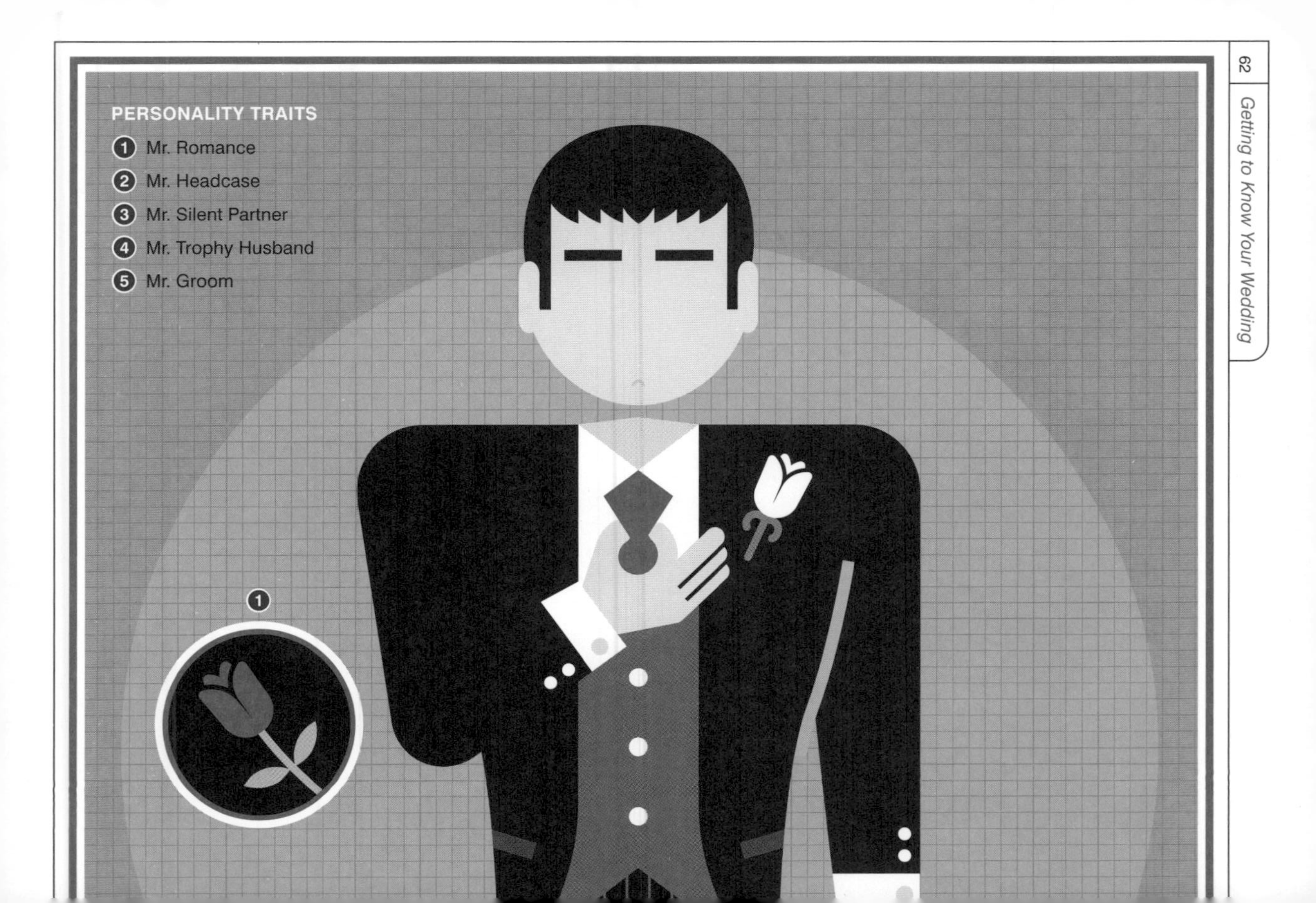
PERSONALITY TRAITS
1 Mr. Romance
2 Mr. Headcase
3 Mr. Silent Partner
4 Mr. Trophy Husband
5 Mr. Groom
1

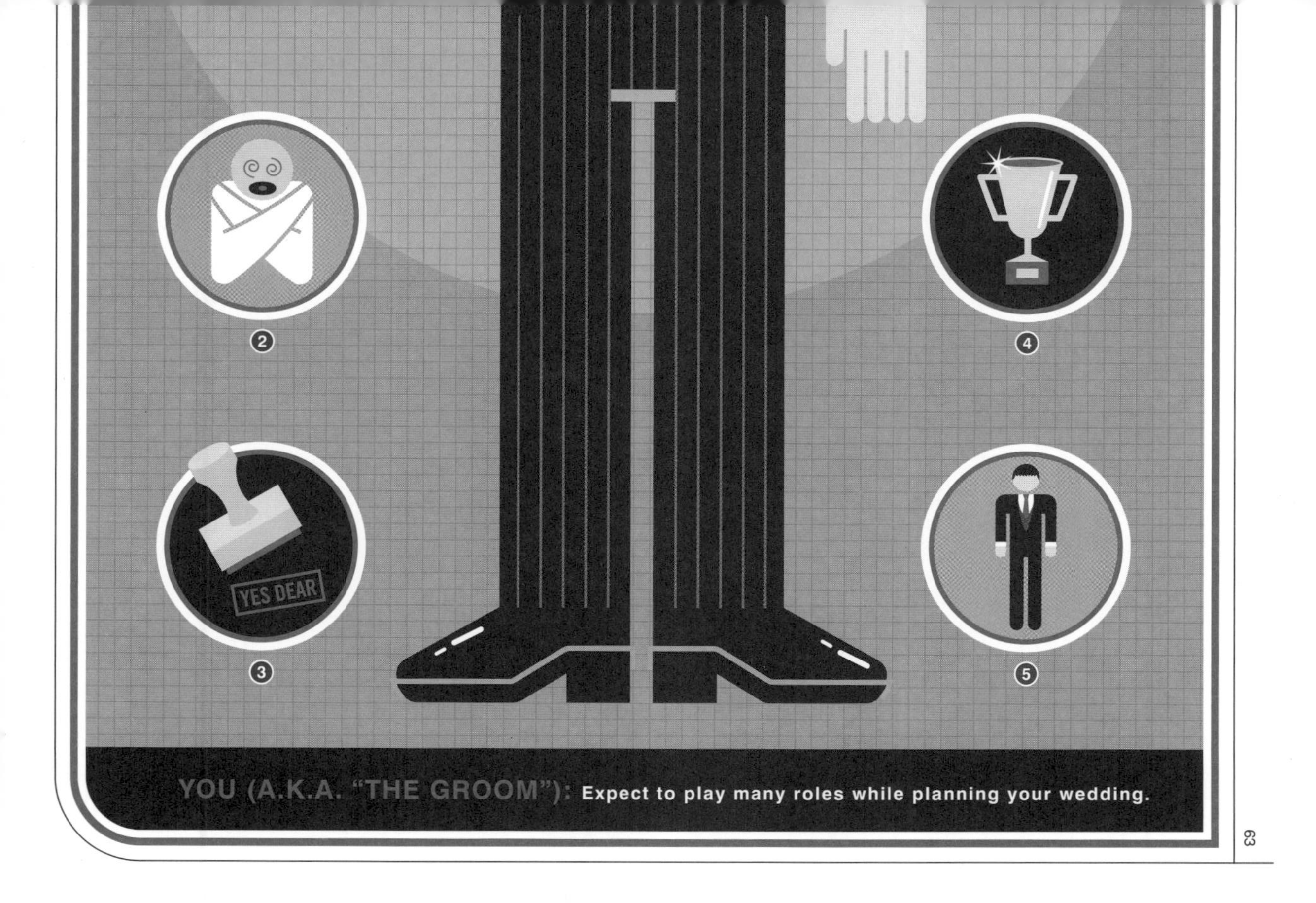

YOU (A.K.A. "THE GROOM"): Expect to play many roles while planning your wedding.

Your Mother-in-Law

Almost without exception, your mother-in-law will be the second-most important woman in the wedding. We don't want to get too dramatic, but it's possible that she will loom over the engagement like an omnipresent and vengeful god. Provided she and your fiancée are on good (or at least speaking) terms, she will be involved in most major decisions for the engagement; she may sign a good percentage of the checks paying for the festivities; and she may even serve as a preview of your wife in the years to come. Ignore her at your own peril.

Personality Traits

■ **Like Daughter, Like Mother.** On some level, we're all a reflection of our parents. When looking for patterns in your mother-in-law's behavior, you should start with your fiancée because, if she has methods for getting her way, it's likely she learned them in part or in whole from mom. The same applies in reverse, so if you get a chance to study how your mother-in-law interacts with your father-in-law, pay attention.

■ **The Ultra-Vicarious Bride.** Your mother-in-law may become so excited by her involvement in the wedding that she may mistake it for her own. She may bring you stacks of dog-eared wedding magazines that are stickered with Post-Its. She may greet your own ideas for the wedding with quiet skepticism. She may get her own wedding dress out of storage and suggest that your fiancée wear it.

She may simply go ahead and make wedding plans without consulting you or your fiancée. If you see any of these telltale signs, you're better off letting your fiancée deal with the situation instead of taking matters into your own hands.

■ **The Executive Assistant.** On the other hand, your mother-in-law may understand her role perfectly, in which case she will be a tremendous asset and ally. In a best-case scenario, your mother-in-law can serve as an extremely professional personal assistant, helping your fiancée narrow down choices on flowers, cakes, venues, and more decisions that you don't want to touch with a ten-foot pole.

■ **The Tradition Cop.** Perhaps you'll be expected to have a strict ceremony for nobody but immediate family. Perhaps you'll be expected to break glasses to cheers of "mazel tov!" Or perhaps you'll be expected to invite the whole damn town where your fiancée grew up. Whatever the expectations, they'll likely be coming from parents, and most often the parent who's most involved in the wedding planning. That's not to say that you and your fiancée will not be amenable to the traditions others hold most dear, but there are bound to be a few that you don't wish to observe. Our advice is to tread lightly—we've said repeatedly that the wedding is about you and your fiancée, but that doesn't mean you get to discount everyone, especially the ones who might be footing the bill. You and your fiancée should figure out which traditions are worth fighting against and which ones aren't, then stand your ground.

MOTHER-IN-LAW
MATERNAL PROTOCOLS
1 Like Daughter, Like Mother
2 The Ultra-Vicarious Bride
3 The Executive Assistant
4 The Tradition Cop
5 The Soon-to-Be Relative
6 The Daughter Agitator
BRIDE
1
2
3
4
5
6

■ **The Soon-to-Be Relative.** The engagement may be just the excuse your mother-in-law was looking for to start telling you what to do. It'll be tough to hold back, but don't fight it too much. Marriage means that soon this woman will officially be your backup mom, so you should treat her with the same respect and dignity with which you would treat your own mother. Except, and here's the hard part, you shouldn't automatically assume that you can argue with her and call her bluff in the same way that you can with your own mother. That'll take some time. But, oh, when that moment comes, cherish it.

■ **The Daughter Agitator.** In some circumstances, your fiancée's mom may be leveling unfair expectations on her daughter's engagement, or she may just be prone to leveling unfair expectations on her daughter in general. You may feel inclined to defend your fiancée's honor. If this moment arises, keep in mind the previous point: What may seem unreasonable to you may just be the way your fiancée and her mom deal with each other, and you don't want to alienate a relative before she's even a relative.

■ **The Uber-Mother.** Finally, count yourself lucky if all the pieces fall into place and your future mother-in-law is that perfect combination of friend, parent, and planner. She may be able to provide great advice based on her experiences rather than her expectations. She may know exactly what it takes to reassure your fiancée. She may even put you perfectly at ease and accept your own requests with open arms. If that happens, you may need this book less than you think.

Your Father-in-Law

Here we have the dynamic in the engagement that has proven most fruitful to Hollywood producers and sitcom writers. It's likely that on some level your fianceé is daddy's little girl and that your future father-in-law was the most important man in her life until you came along. Leave it to the wedding gods to designate that the man who will very likely hold the purse strings to your celebration of matrimony is the same man who will be most dubious of your intentions.

Why is he so suspicious of you? Because he's a guy—he was once in your shoes and he sees in you how clueless he once was. If you can tear yourself away from the anxiety, you may actually learn something about yourself in your dealings with your fiancée's dad.

Personality Traits

■ **Her Protector.** Since the day your fiancée was born, her father has possessed a primal instinct to protect his daughter against all hostilities. He's probably seen a couple boyfriends before you, and, whether he's the kind of guy to offer a beer and some advice or a shotgun barrel and the door, he wants what's best for his little girl. By the time you're engaged, we hope you and your future father-in-law will have formed some kind of relationship. But be on notice that when his money is involved and when his daughter is in a more consistent state of excitement, he'll likewise be on his guard. Your best way to reassure him is to reassure your fiancée.

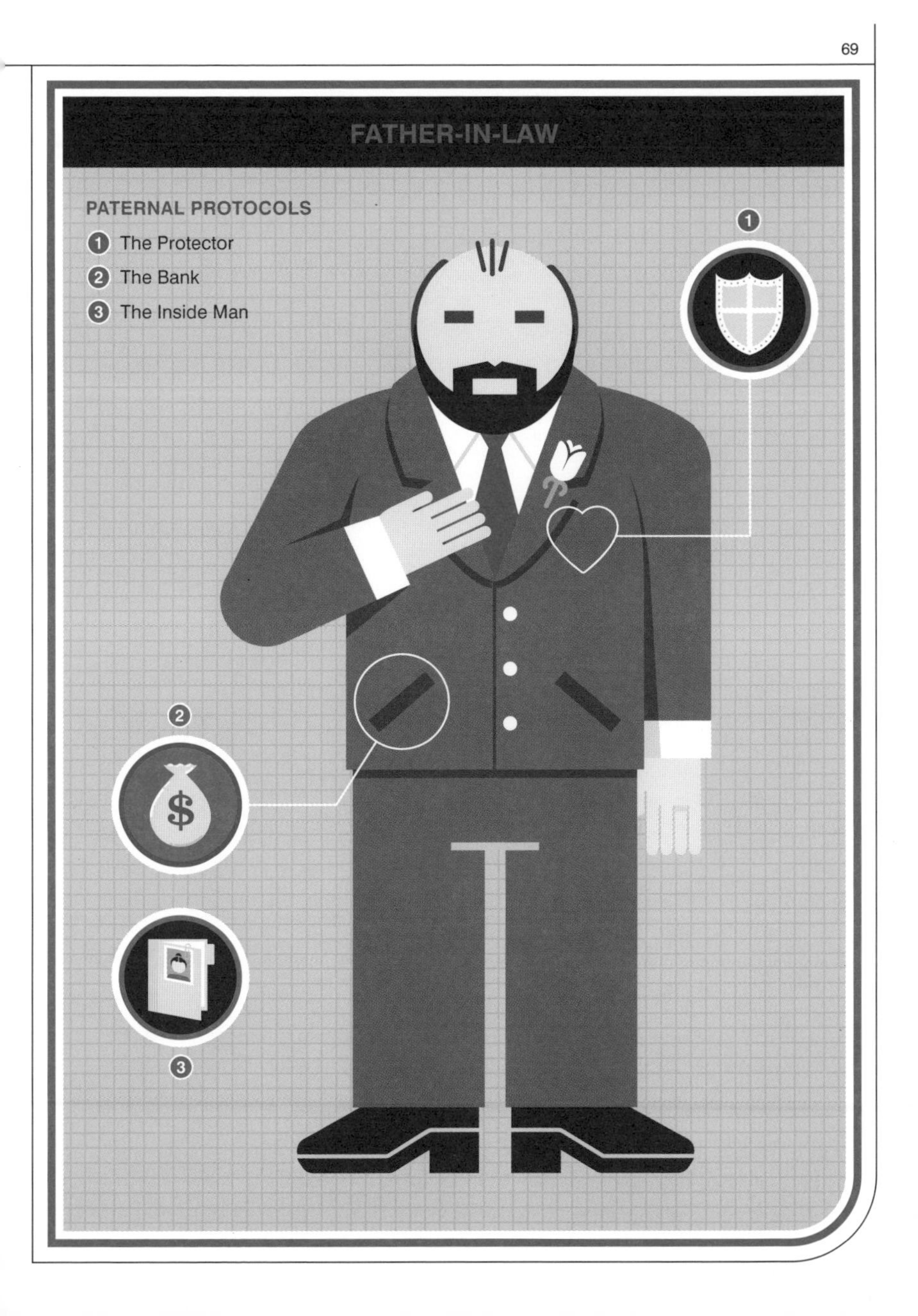
FATHER-IN-LAW
PATERNAL PROTOCOLS
1 The Protector
2 The Bank
3 The Inside Man
1
2
3

- **The Bank.** It could be that you and your fiancée will be shouldering the majority of the costs for the wedding, or that costs will be equally distributed among both families. But if your wedding is financed in a traditional manner, the majority of the invoices will be signed by your dear old (fiancée's) dad. So, don't anger him by overspending—and, under this "traditional" financial arrangement, you should defer to your fiancée anyway (whew).

- **The Inside Man.** Another reason that you want to cultivate a great relationship with your future father-in-law is because he may be able to provide you with not only insights to your fiancée but moral support. After all, he's known his daughter her whole life, so in most cases he can probably sense what's on her mind. During trying times, he can even provide a voice of reason or a calming presence. However, don't be fooled into believing that because you guys are buddies, he'll automatically be on board to help you out if things get heavy. His first priority is still his daughter, so when you're the one who screws up, you're still on your own.

Your Mother

Your mother fills a unique role: She is the most prominent woman involved in the wedding whose participation is completely expendable. Of course, you must never, never, never acknowledge this fact to your mother. In a lot of cases, your wedding may be the most excitement she's had since, well, her wedding.

Personality Traits

■ **Your Protector.** Over the course of the wedding, your mother may kick into a natural protective mode if she feels that your fiancée or anybody else is taking advantage of you. How your mother chooses to approach this dilemma will have a monumental impact on the dynamic between the woman who gave birth to you and the woman with whom you plan to spend the rest of your life. You may soon face the twin tasks of protecting your mother's feelings while assuring your wife that she is the Number One woman in your life. Don't make us tell you who is more important and who will get over it sooner.

■ **The Vicarious Bride.** As with your mother-in-law, your own mother may stumble into the trap of mistaking your wedding for her own. Watch for the warning signs discussed above (see pages 64–65).

■ **The Rehearsal Dinner Planner.** Wedding rituals in the Western world allow the groom's family a chance to plan a special mini-event of their own: the rehearsal dinner. We'll describe this to-do in more detail later; for now, consider it a shiny plaything to distract your mother (and possibly father) from the fact that she is not making major decisions about the wedding itself.

Your Father

Dads are confidants of a different sort. If you have a good relationship with your father, he can say all of the wise and witty

things that make sons feel good about themselves and provide valuable insight about what the wedding will truly mean to you. Even better, we can absolutely guarantee that he won't butt in with his opinion about the flower arrangements.

Personality Traits

■ **The Consigliere.** As your confidante, Mom helps you figure out your emotions. As your consigliere, Dad helps you turn your emotions into action items. And you'll need that action to get through both the bad stuff and the really bad stuff. Dad will take what you're feeling and be able to point you in the right direction.

■ **The Battle-Tested Soldier.** Unless your parents have had an unnaturally perfect marriage, your father has seen some serious, ahem, female behavior in his day. At a minimum, he made it through a wedding—or possibly several. And whether you want to admit it or not, your mother likely shares many traits with your fiancée. In other words, your dad can speak very clearly about what you need to do to alleviate any potentially volatile situations. But beware . . .

■ **The War-Torn Veteran.** What may sound like advice could subconsciously be your father's summation of what he wished he'd done if he'd had the guts.

■ **The Man Inaction.** It's possible that your dad can be your hero and also be the lazy guy who watches TV and ignores everyone in the house to avoid confrontation. Plus, generational differences can be profound

YOUR PARENTS
MATERNAL PROTOCOLS
1 Rehearsal Dinner Planner
2 Your Protector
PATERNAL PROTOCOLS
3 The Consigliere
4 The Battle-Tested Soldier
1
2
3
4

when it comes to marriages, so your role in your own wedding may be truly foreign to him. It may be that he just can't provide you much help beyond moral support, in which case you should gladly take what you can get and turn to your groomsmen for the heavy lifting.

The Best Man

Picking the man who stands at your side on your wedding day may be a foregone conclusion. You may have known since childhood that it would be your brother or your dad or your best friend. But now that the time has come to choose, you might want to review the decision, because a solid best man can make the difference between enjoying (or at least enduring) the engagement to the fullest or barely surviving it on your own.

Personality Traits

■ **A True Friend.** Your best man is not just someone you can trust to plan an entertaining bachelor party. He should be the rare kind of guy you can talk to about your feelings. If that isn't something you're used to doing, don't expect that he can learn the necessary skills "on the job." Instead, make sure your frontrunner is qualified from the beginning before you offer him the gig.

■ **An Able Courier.** As the wedding day approaches, you'll be amazed at how much you need to do. In these situations, you'll need to lean on your best man to get things done. Make sure he's willing and able to help. That may mean you should pick somebody who's geographically available, though in the Internet age, geography may not matter as much as simple availability.

■ **An Iceman.** When you're freaking out, the last thing you need is a best man who's throwing coals on the fire. Try to find one who can talk you down from any ledge.

■ **A Joiner.** Although you want a best man to whom you can turn for good advice, what you really need is somebody who knows when to offer advice and when to simply restate what you think differently enough so that it *seems* like advice. In other words, a maid of honor who has contradictory opinions about your wedding should be dealt with; a best man with contradictory opinions about your wedding should be amputated.

■ **A Mensch.** It's the Yiddish word for "human being," and for all of the reasons listed here, you're well advised to select one for your best man.

Personality Traits to Avoid

■ **A Drinkin' Buddy.** If you're under the age of twenty-five, read this paragraph very carefully. What may seem like a smashing friendship now may actually just be a partnership in crime. Make sure you like your best man as much sober as drunk, because marriage is a sobering experience.

■ **A Yin to Your Yang.** What may work in life may not work in engagement. Just because you're quiet and studious doesn't mean you

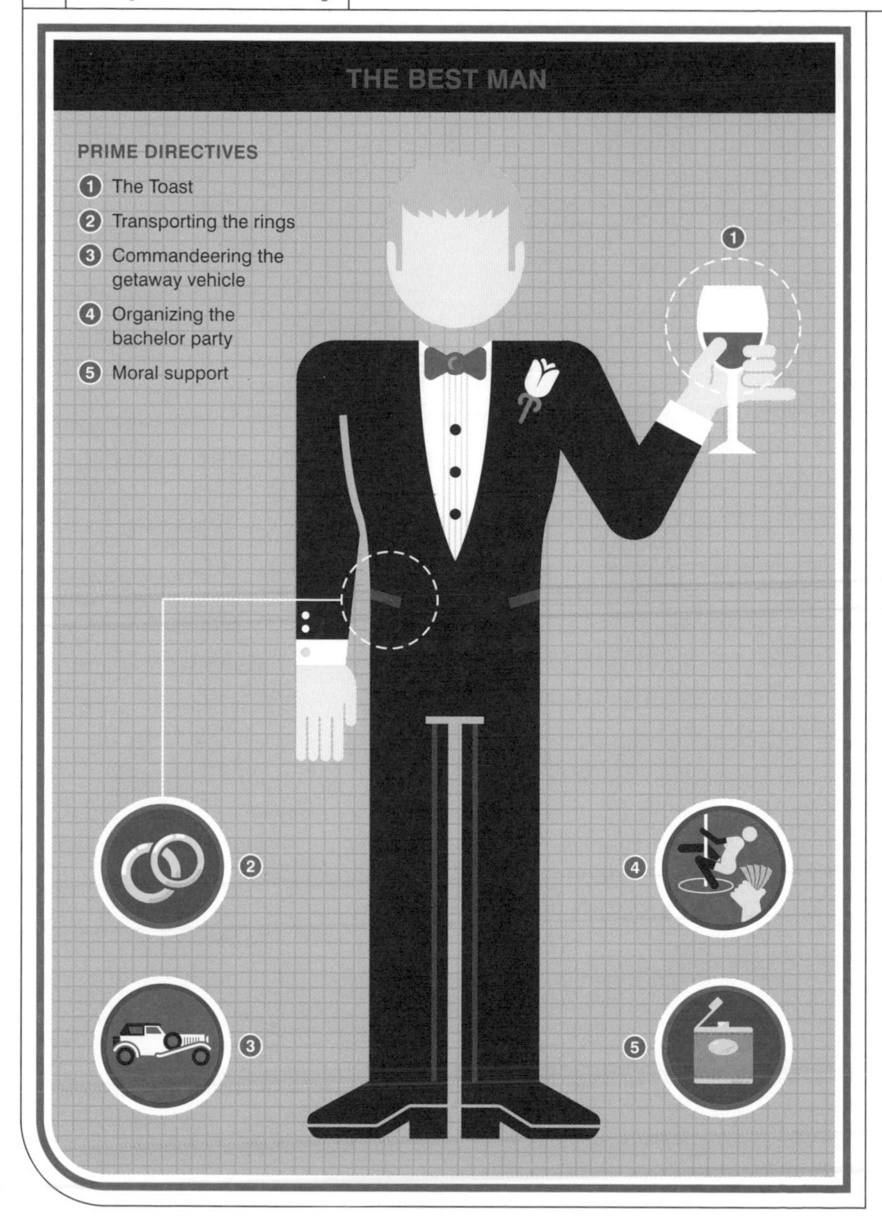
THE BEST MAN
PRIME DIRECTIVES
1 The Toast
2 Transporting the rings
3 Commandeering the getaway vehicle
4 Organizing the bachelor party
5 Moral support
1
2
3
4
5

should designate your life-of-the-party friend as your best man, for he may have no interest in being second banana.

■ **A Political Appointment.** Don't let anyone force you into a selection. Apart from proposing to your fiancée, your choice of a best man is one that you alone will know how to make, so don't let family or friends treat it as a job open for applications.

■ **A Heckler.** This one may be tough to recognize until it's too late. Basically, if you have a friend who really makes you laugh, but it's usually at the expense of others, you'll want to keep yourself from becoming an "other."

Potential Best Men

■ **Your Father.** Tradition and/or your own feelings may dictate that your father will stand by your side, which will make your decision easy. Just remember that Dad may be distracted with other wedding responsibilities (friends arriving from out of town and so on). It's also unlikely that your father will arrange the kind of bachelor party that can land you and your buddies in prison. Whether you see that as a plus or a minus depends on your personal taste.

■ **Your Brother.** If you and your brother are close, he makes another excellent choice. Just watch out for sibling rivalries or other contentious episodes that may get in the way of your being a groom. A wedding is a great time to grow the bond between you and your brother, but it could be an awful time to find out how immature it already is.

■ **Your Best Friend.** This decision may be a foregone conclusion, but if it's not, have a complimentary answer ready for those who felt like they should've been selected as your best man but weren't.

Groomsmen

The groomsmen can be thought of as your entourage. They will help you with certain things during the engagement and at the wedding, but for the most part they will be there to provide you safety in numbers, to feed you dollar bills at your bachelor party, and to have a good time of their own at your reception. All they have to do is wear the right suit and hit their cues on the big day, and in return they get to be mini-celebrities at your celebration. These are, in many respects, political appointments, and you get to play Mr. President.

Considerations

Your criteria for your groomsmen don't need to be as strict as those for your best man, but you're well advised to at least consider several of the points listed above. In addition, look out for these suggestions:

■ **Consult the future missus.** You get to make the decisions, but don't think you can do so without consulting your fiancée. She shouldn't have veto power except in extreme circumstances (for example, personal history between her and one of your choices), but it's good for her to hear and understand your selection.

■ **Size matters.** If your fiancée is only asking her three sisters to be bridesmaids, you should probably limit yourself to three groomsmen—there's something about symmetry that makes those wedding photos look good. By the same token, if your fiancée plans on having a dozen bridesmaids, you may need to start calling old college friends you haven't spoken to in years.

■ **Money matters.** If you plan on covering any expenses for your bridesmaids and groomsmen (travel arrangements, clothes, accommodations), you'll want to take that into account before you start asking people.

■ **Crews can't lose.** If you have a group of friends—the funny one, the fat one, the smart one, and so on—who are always together and always have a great time, make 'em your groomsmen. You'll appreciate the familiarity.

Bridesmaids

You won't have a whole lot to do with the bridesmaids, so we'll just offer two pieces of advice.

First, don't sleep with them. Such an infelicity won't be looked upon with admiration by your fiancée or anyone else, except perhaps your groomsmen. If you've previously slept with any of them, don't draw attention to that fact because, even if your fiancée knows and is fine with it, the increased pressure of a wedding can quickly turn any skeletons in your closet into a dangerous liability.

Second, use them to your advantage. Just as your groomsmen are your temporary handlers, the bridesmaids are there for your fiancée throughout the engagement. If you need information from your fiancée but can't ask her directly, try working through one of her bridesmaids.

Wedding Planners

It's becoming more and more common to supplement the planning of the bride, mother-in-law, and other relatives with the skills of trained wedding professionals. Good wedding planners will make it easier for your fiancée to create the wedding of her dreams, thus making it easier for you to sit back and enjoy the engagement. They'll follow her lead and take care of the little details, providing direction and suggestions as needed. And, of course, they also charge an arm and a leg.

You'll have very little involvement when a wedding planner is doing a good job, other than to follow her or his cues for when to provide moral support and second opinions.

Traits of a Good Wedding Planner

- **The planner asks a lot of questions.** Such interest indicates that the planner is trying to understand whims and desires unique to you and your fiancée—and is not merely applying her standard template to your event. Similarly . . .

- **The planner respects your wishes.** If you've made it clear that you want a country-western band at your wedding, the planner shouldn't be pushing you to consider jazz, swing, or chamber music.

■ **The planner understands and respects your budget.** He or she should ask early on what you would like to spend and then determine if he or she can afford to work on your event. Unexpected costs are bound to pop up along the way, but a good wedding planner won't pressure you to consider dozens of costly add-ons.

■ **The planner won't be fazed by an occasional meltdown.** Few people have seen as many extremes of human behavior as professional wedding planners, and these people are paid to shoulder your burdens. So if your fiancée bursts into tears during a discussion about floral arrangements, the planner should console her and explain that tearful outbursts are normal during the engagement process.

A bad wedding planner won't do anything worthwhile, will charge exorbitant fees, or will likely impose his or her own expectations on the wedding. Depending on her disposition, your fiancée may be more easily suggestible during her engagement than she would be otherwise, so what seems absurd to you may start looking like a no-brainer to her. If that happens, you may need to intervene. Look for these signs of bad planning:

Traits of a Bad Wedding Planner

■ **Your fiancée feels overwhelmed by everything the planner has asked her to do—including such tasks as calling venues to confirm**

availability. Wedding planners are supposed to help relieve the stress by taking care of the small things.

- **Your fiancée's dream wedding is slowly supplanted by a version of the wedding you've heard the wedding planner promote.** Some planners are really just egomaniacs who can't see beyond their own agenda. If you see the planner taking over in a bad way, make sure your fiancée sees it, too.

- **Your fiancée argues with your wedding planner about major and minor details.** In some cases, it will be your fiancée's quest for perfection that is driving these arguments. But be sure to keep an eye out to see if the wedding planner is just combative and generally demanding.

- **Costs for the wedding start to balloon thanks to changes of venue and vendor, upon the planner's suggestion.** If your planner claims to have sweetheart deals, make sure they're just that and that you're not being abused by a wedding services cabal.

- **Your planner is openly arrogant and combative about her or his vision and planning prowess.** Remember, this person is an event planner, not a tortured genius, so don't let him or her act that way. In dire situations, don't hesitate to fire a wedding planner, even if it means that the wedding will need to be reconceived as a much smaller (and less complicated) event.

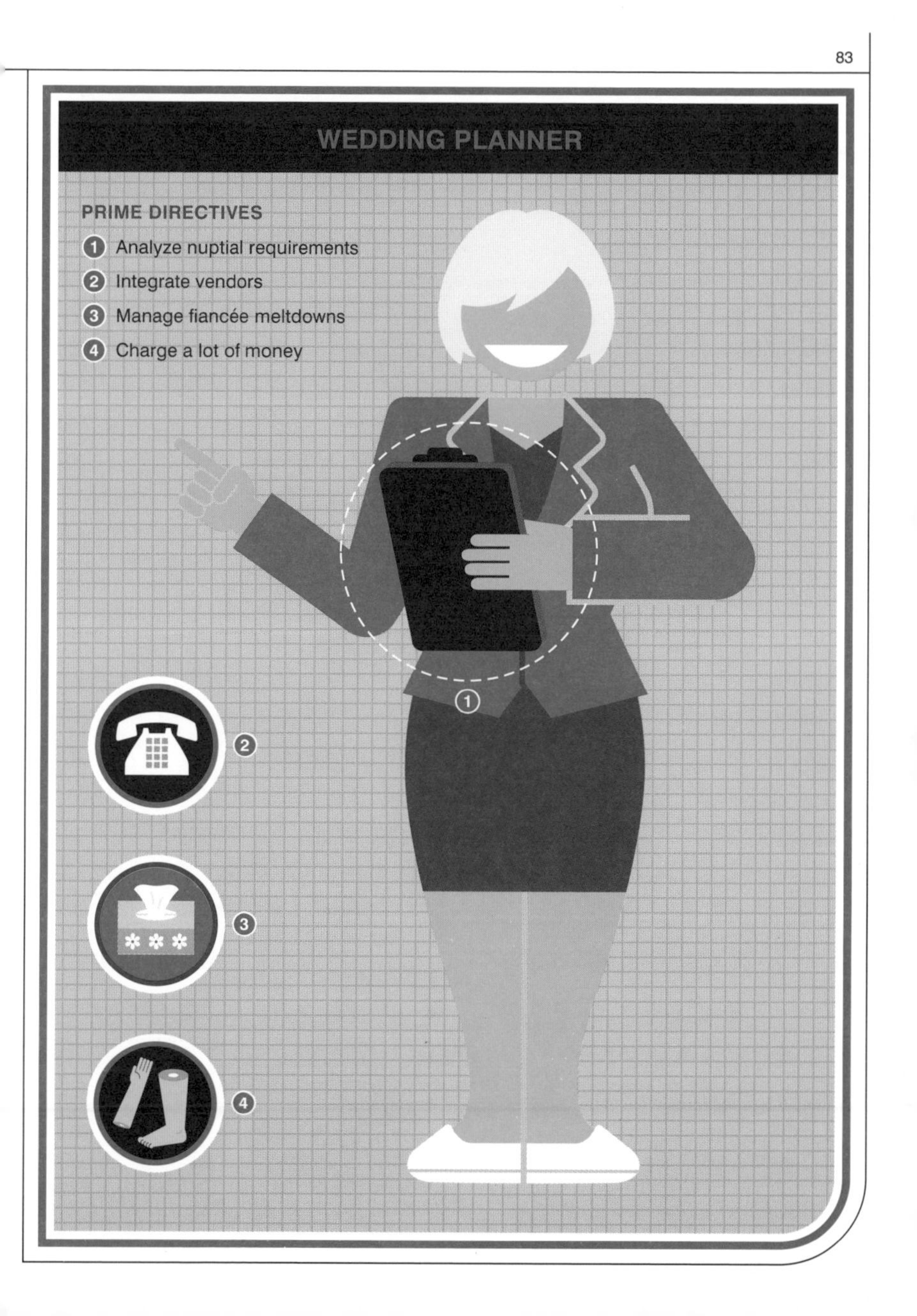
WEDDING PLANNER
PRIME DIRECTIVES
1 Analyze nuptial requirements
2 Integrate vendors
3 Manage fiancée meltdowns
4 Charge a lot of money
1
2
3
4

The Officiant

The officiant will make your matrimony official—hence the name. He or she will ask you if you take your fiancée, if she takes you, til death do you part, yadda, yadda, yadda. This person could be a priest, rabbi, rector, or other religious figure at your preferred house of worship; your favorite judge or justice of the peace; or someone you found in the phone book when you checked in to your motel. Whoever it is, there's more to deciding who will marry you than simply being qualified to officiate, so make sure you pick wisely.

Religious Officiants

For the vast majority of engaged couples, the officiant will be a religious figure. If you or your fiancée have a favorite preacher from your youth or from your current place of worship, your decision will be easy. Otherwise, keep a few things in mind.

- **Are you right with God's people?** A wedding reception is not Sunday service. Places of worship can and will say no if they feel you don't meet their requirements for tying the knot. These requirements can be as simple as not belonging to their congregation (important if you plan a destination wedding at a church) and can be as detailed as your sexual history. So if you're dealing with an officiant for the first time, be prepared for what may seem like a surprisingly probing interrogation.

- **Are you a traditionalist?** In most major religions, the ceremonial traditions culminating in marriage are centuries and even millennia old, and they're not usually open to reinvention. In the Christian faith, most ceremonies involve some sort of sacrament and readings, usually from the Bible. In the Jewish faith, you will be expected to raise a veil from your bride's face before reading the *Ketubah* (marriage contract) and saying your vows under the *Huppah* (wedding canopy). Other faiths have their own traditions that cannot be altered. So, if you always planned on serenading your lady with that song you wrote in junior high, or if you planned to have cousin Rob practice his marriage bit before the vows, you'll want to check with the officials at your place of worship before you get the ball rolling.

■ **Mi casa ain't su casa.** And if you think you'll get out of the traditions because you're getting married on the beach instead of on the pulpit, think again. You can take the preacher out of the house of God, but don't expect to take the house of God out of the preacher.

■ **Religion lite is available.** Don't get too concerned if you'd like to have faith without the fanfare. You can find open-minded congregations that will provide a modicum of religious tradition combined with less strict rules on what you can do with your vows, readings, ritual sacrifices, and more. You may just have to look a little harder and be open to alternate venues.

Official Officiants

Throughout the United States, a low-level adjudicator called a justice of the peace can solemnize marriages. They're typically used for quickie marriages down at city hall, in which case you may get the romantic bonus of having the person recite your vows from behind a Plexiglas shield. However, certain justices of the peace may provide a more traditional wedding ceremony sans religious overtones. If you and your fiancée are set on keeping religion 100 percent out of your ceremony, you should contact your local county government or search the Internet for justices of the peace in your area.

Official for a Day

Depending on where you plan to get married, you may find the right officiant within your own family or circle of friends. Several states will allow people with no professional experience to perform officially recognized wedding ceremonies. Having a friend or family member act as your officiant could make your wedding seem extra-special and unique, but take note:

- **Make sure it's legal.** There's no greater letdown after the pomp and circumstance of a marriage ceremony than to schlep down to city hall and have your bonds made official by said Plexiglas justice of the peace because you or your friend didn't read the fine print on his or her licensing rules. Get everything squared away well before the big day.

- **Can this person work a room?** Perhaps you want somebody who means a lot to you and your fiancée to perform the ceremony. Problem is, that person comes off like driftwood in front of crowds. Your wedding will likely be a very public, very pressure-cooked event, and you may not truly appreciate a lively emcee who will keep the show going

SELECTING AN OFFICIANT
Consult your spiritual service provider, but yield to your fiancée if possible.

until you don't have one. On the other hand, you may know the perfect extroverted friend who will totally kill. Just make sure she or he knows that this is your wedding and not open-mic night at Club Bananas.

- **Practice, practice, practice.** It may be hard to predict how your friend-officiant will perform under pressure. To keep everything on track and avoid surprises, walk through the ceremony several times before the big day so that your officiant has a good idea of what will be expected and so that you and your fiancée have a good idea of what the officiant will do.

Wildcards

All weddings have their regulars, and virtually all weddings have their irregulars. Don't worry, it's bound to happen when you're bringing together friends and family from two different worlds. Some people you'll be able to stop; others you should just be happy to contain.

Drunken Relatives

Offering free alcohol to people who can't handle liquor isn't a great idea—and yet it happens at every wedding. In most situations, all you'll have to deal with are stories from incredulous and/or highly amused friends about Cousin Albert's horrifyingly graphic dance number. In fact, one of the great thrills of hosting a wedding reception is talking to others about all of the strange hookups, letdowns, and embarrassments that happened while you were meeting and greeting other guests.

But, if you have reason to believe that a guest will slip well past the threshold of minor embarrassment, you must work through other relatives (or friends) to prevent the situation. Under most circumstances, this task will be much easier with friends than with family because you can cross an embarrassing friend off the guest list. With family, such steps can have major repercussions. But, here's your one opportunity to put down your foot and worry about the consequences later—it's your wedding and you shouldn't let it be spoiled simply because the guy you can't take anywhere might be offended when he doesn't get an invitation. Plenty of people will tell you that you can't dis family like that, but keep in mind that family shouldn't be able to dis you on your wedding day, either.

Ex-Girlfriends and Ex-Boyfriends

Almost all of us have them, and some of us are still (appropriately) friendly with them. But if you or your fiancée plans to invite an ex or exes to the wedding, don't be surprised if one of them tries to steal a kiss or cut in while you're dancing. See, love is already in the air, and when you factor in that you're going to look like James Bond and your fiancée will look like every tenth-grader's sexual fantasy, your exes may have some old feelings resurface. Add an open bar and voilà! What's old is new again.

Unsupervised Children

We love children at weddings. Really, we do. They always get an "Awwww" when they're walking down the aisle throwing rose petals to and fro. Unfortunately, some kids have trouble taking direction. So while your fiancée is making plans to have her niece bring the rings up the aisle on a silk pillow, make your own plans to assure there's somebody watching the kid so that the rings don't end up in a very small nostril.

Unsupervised Grandparents

We love grandparents at weddings, too. Just remember that they tend to move slowly. So, as you're making some of your logistical plans, think about whether your grandparents will be in attendance and, if so, what might need to be modified so that they can enjoy the festivities as much as everyone else.

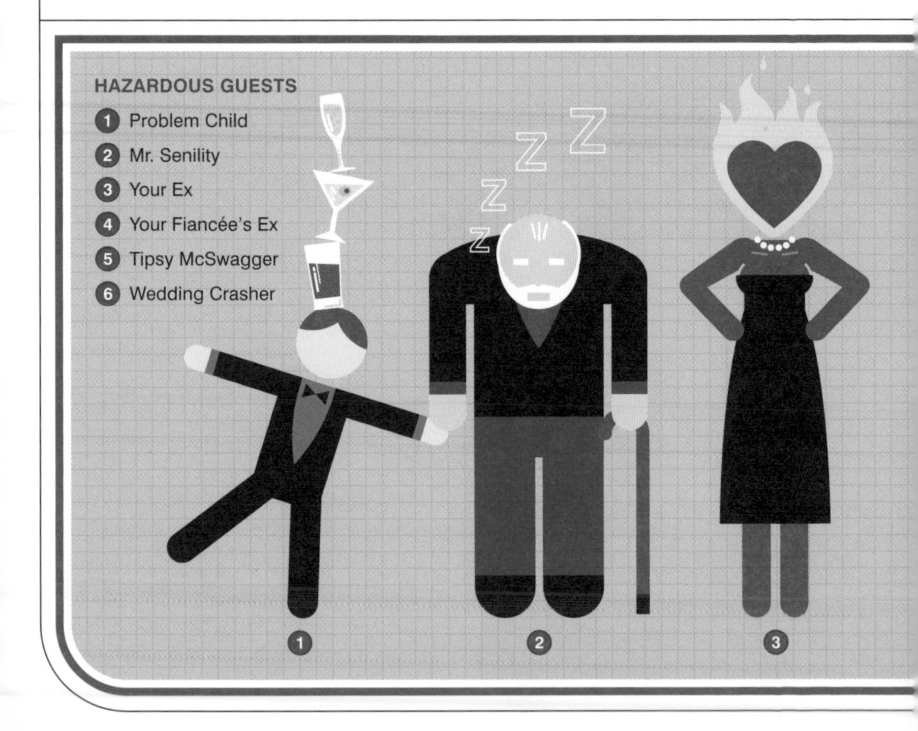

Uninvited Guests

There's a science to compiling your guest list. Yet, inevitably, you'll get some people who don't bother to RSVP, and others who don't indicate that they're bringing guests. On the wedding day, your public attitude should be the same as it was for house parties in college—the more, the merrier. But do what you can prior to the event to make it clear to your friends (men are usually the ones who need the most direction) whether their invitation will allow them to bring dates.

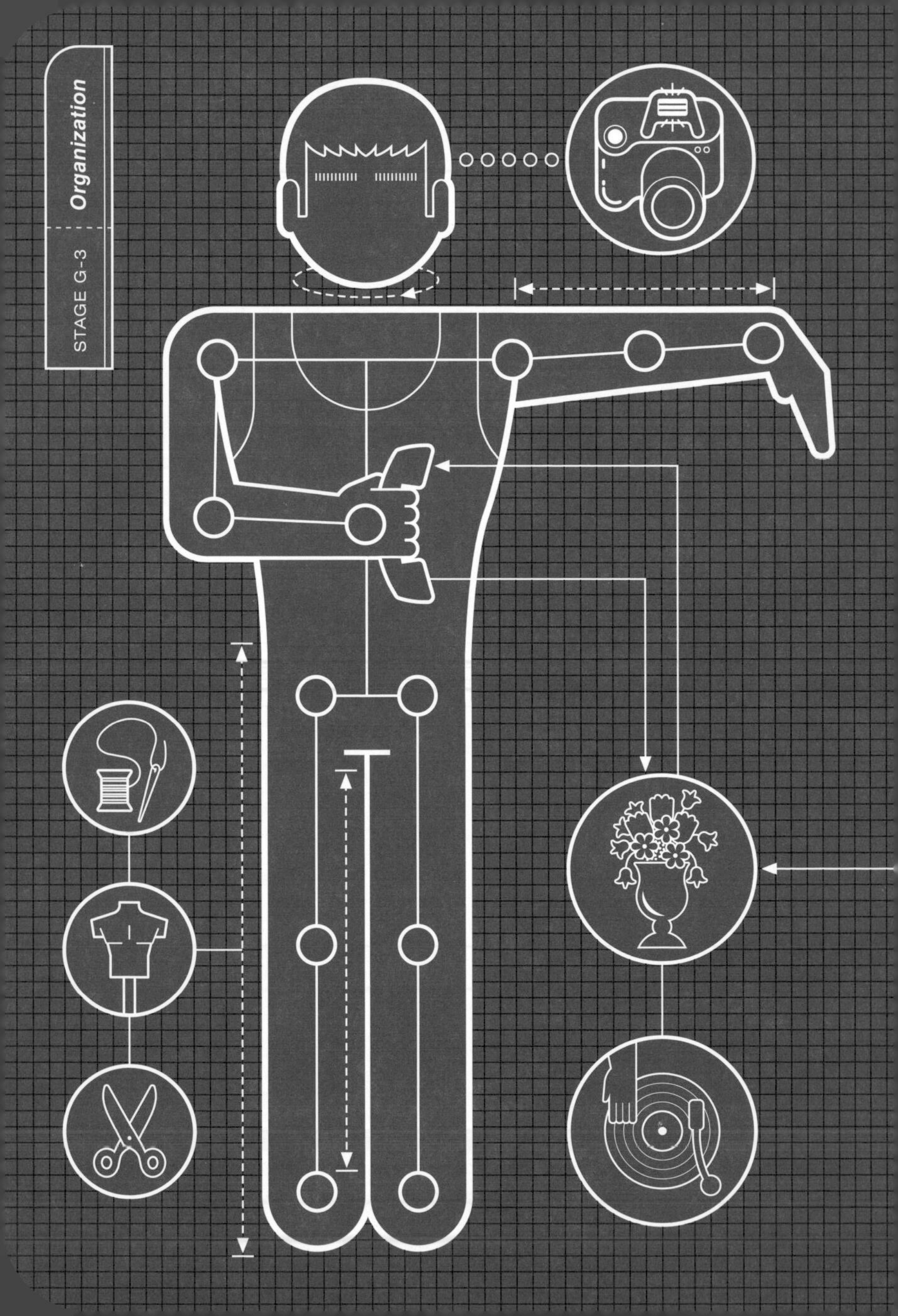
Organization
STAGE G-3

[Chapter 3]

The Engagement

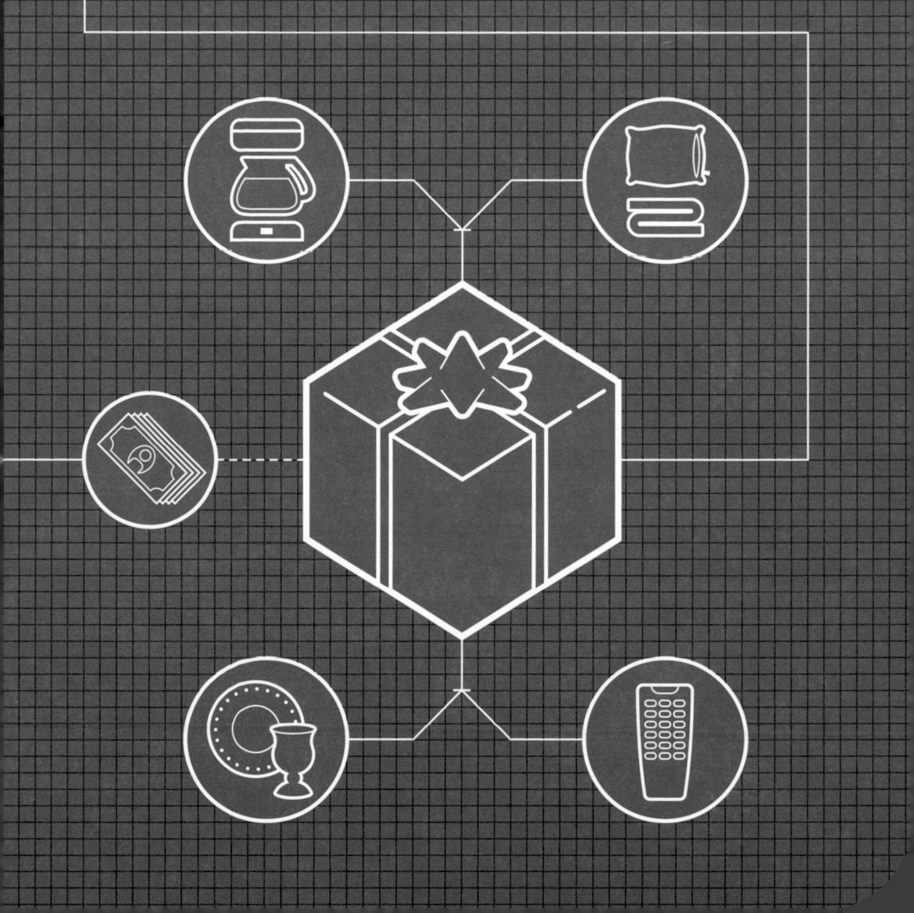

Congratulations. You've made it this far into the wedding planning without encountering any gratuitous sports analogies—until now. Reading the previous chapter was like "watching film"—you now understand the players you will meet on the field. But the engagement is not, as you may think, the Big Game. It is instead the two-a-day practices that will leave you energized on some days and so battered on other days that you'll want to tape bags of ice to your thighs to relieve the swelling. Now get out there and play ball!

Drafting the Guest List

Coming up with an invitation list for the wedding should be easy. You sit down with your fiancée and your respective contact lists, you determine how many people can come, you prioritize and make your list, you inform your parents of your decisions, and then you celebrate with peanuts and boilermakers. Oh, if only . . .

Actually, the guest list may be possibly the one logistical task that will prompt demands from both the bride and groom, both mothers, and, potentially, both fathers. Yet, like dueling diplomats unsure of what the other is bringing to the bargaining table, your parents will likely never be in the same room for these discussions. Instead, you and your fiancée will act as representatives for your respective families. That's right, you will be a messenger for your own wedding, relaying information without revealing too much, and all the while trying to convince yourself that the wedding still belongs to you. To ease the process, remember:

Ceremony ≠ Reception

The wedding ceremony and the wedding reception are usually two separate events. They may be held at the same place, and the reception will almost certainly be right after the ceremony, but all your guests will not necessarily attend both events. Check with your fiancée about capacity issues, and keep in mind that your most valued guests will almost always attend your ceremony—unless you plan a very small service that will include only your immediate family.

Make a Budget, Make a Plan, Stick to Both

There's a phrase that you should get used to hearing in the coming months: cost per head. Roughly translated, this can be thought of as the average cost of all reception-related expenses—food, beverages, venue—for each person. Even though you'll want to keep the wedding as personal and fun as possible, you need to attach a dollar value to everyone who walks through the door. The cost per head alone may be all the motivation you need to carve up your guest list like a Thanksgiving turkey. We encourage you to remember this wonderful advice that a mother-in-law once shared: Weddings aren't about how many friends are attending, they're about how much food and drink they get to enjoy at the reception. In other words, fewer well-fed, well-lit friends will make for a grander wedding than hungrier, more sober ones.

Know Your Place

Since helping with the guest list will likely be the opening salvo to your substantive involvement in the wedding, it's a good opportunity to establish how you plan to be involved. If you really couldn't care less, just hand over to your fiancée your list and your parents' list and let her do with them what she will. If you do have strong opinions about the guest list, you'll have to put your foot down. But . . .

If You Put Your Foot Down, Know What You're Stepping In

It's possible that somebody you're ready to do battle over really isn't that close of a friend or that your wife has legitimate reasons for not wanting that person there. The same can work in reverse, of course.

You Are Not Your Parents

Remember that you're making a list of people you want at your wedding. Your respective parents will likely weigh more heavily, yet unconsciously, on the guest list than in any other area of the wedding. But it's still your and your fiancée's day, so join forces and don't let your parents forget it.

Punish the Hard Sell

For once in your life, you get to be the bouncer at the velvet

rope. You may not get to decide everyone who gets to be there, but you can have a fair amount of say about who doesn't get to be there. If someone is harassing you about an invitation but you hadn't seriously considered them for the list, stick with your instincts. It may lead to some hard feelings—but if you don't want this person at your wedding, you don't need to sweat him.

The Invitees

Now that you know how to make your choices, learn how your choices can be classified.

The Mandatories: These are your most important guests—typically family members and close friends. You should know who your mandatories are—for example, a college roommate probably isn't mandatory on his own merits, but a college roommate who's a best friend deserves to make the cut. As for family, if you have a large one, you should always err on the side of inviting people.

The Parentals: Your parents and your fiancée's parents will likely submit their own lists of "mandatories." If you're lucky, their lists will be limited primarily to people who are already covered in your own lists of mandatories. But don't bank on it. If your mother is prone to telling the whole world that there's a wedding coming up, and her little boy is the main attraction, you may have to force her to make some tough choices.

Depending on how close you and your parents are emotionally and geographically, their list may include friends and neighbors who know you very well despite never having met you, thanks to your parents' stories about you. Or they may be people you haven't seen since your were a child. Your parents may think of these people as mandatory, but if you're on a budget or pushing the limit, they're absolutely not. Of course, if your fiancée's family is footing the bill, this point will be difficult for you to argue; we suggest you work with your fiancée to discover a compromise that seems fair to both families.

Seat Fillers: If you get your Mandatories and Parentals out of the way and find that you're not wiped out, go ahead and invite the people you'd really like to have at your wedding but whose attendance you don't consider mandatory.

The Compromises: Filling the final 25 percent of your guest list is a bit like selecting a jury. You'll want to take into account the considerations and classifications outlined above and then negotiate with your fiancée and/or family. You may even want to limit all parties to a set amount of vetoes, just so you can get through the list before the wedding itself comes and goes.

The Registry Fillers: As a logical, progressive-thinking male, you might think it odd to invite a person who, in all likelihood, will probably not attend your wedding. Yet there are two compelling reasons to do so. First, this person will certainly appreciate the gesture—everyone likes an invitation. Second, they might demonstrate their appreciation by purchasing an item from your registry. Does that seem rather cold and calculating? Of course it does. But we never said that planning a wedding would be a walk in the park.

Put Your Left-Brain Logic to Work

For all you left-brain thinkers out there, compiling a guest list is the perfect opportunity to show off your logistical prowess. Create a chart or sorting system that groups your invitees into several key categories: Mandatories, Parentals, Seat Fillers, Compromises, and Registry Fillers. Next, apply rankings based on relation, emotional connection, fun factor, and gift-giving potential, and see how your list turns out. Ranking your friends and family in this manner can be an eye-opening experience—but don't be surprised if your fiancée's opinions contrast sharply with your own.

The Consequences

Once your list has been set and your invitations sent, you're bound to find out that you missed some people and/or misjudged the people who did make the list. This is normal—it's pretty tough to get a list with so many variables right the first time around. Just save enough invitations and figure enough into your budget so that you can fix the mistakes when they happen.

Drafting the Guest List

Photocopy the form below and complete one for each first, and then by their "★" rating. Use these ratings

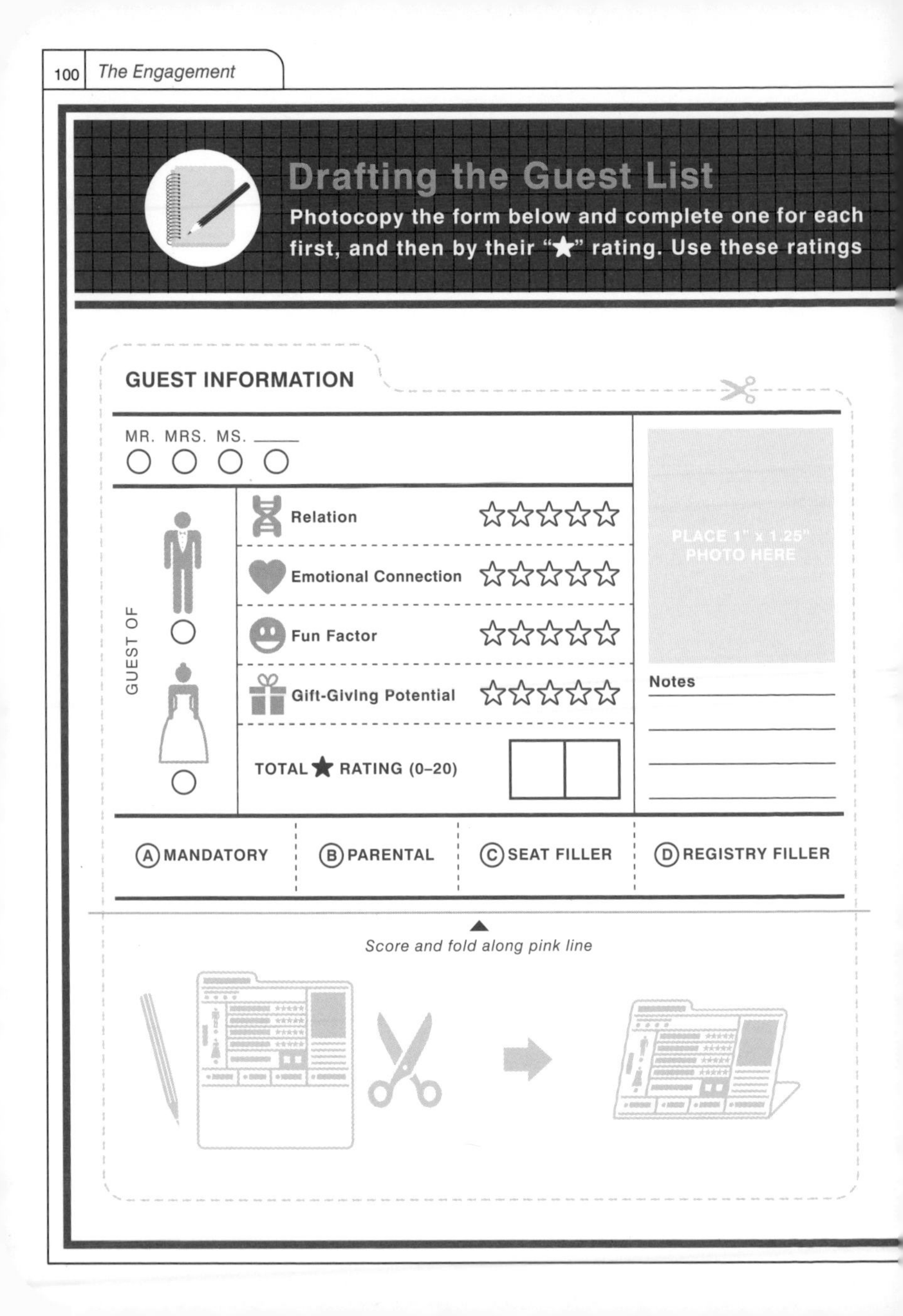

of your potential guests. Sort them into Categories A through D to determine who makes the final cut and who does not.

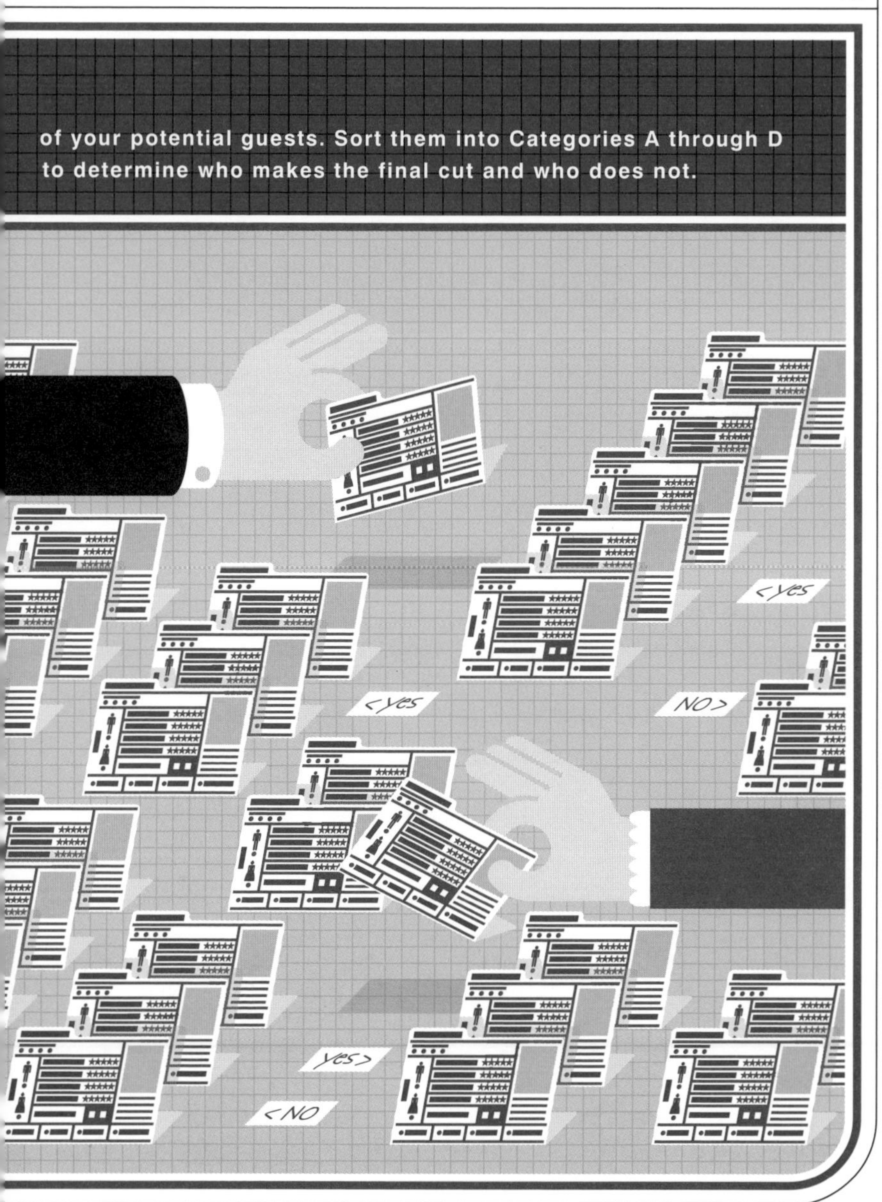

Drafting a Seating Chart

If you plan to serve any kind of sit-down meal at your reception, it's probably best to figure out where your guests should sit. Your fiancée may relish this task because it's the perfect opportunity for her to play matchmaker—at long last, her shy cousin from Boise can finally meet your old college roommate, the Silicon Valley venture capitalist. Let your fiancée have her fun, but try to remember the following concerns:

Seat the Wedding Party Together

All bridesmaids, groomsmen, immediate family members, and other members of the wedding party should receive preferred seating near the front of the venue (or at the wedding-party table if you plan to have one).

Seat Your Friends with Your Friends, and Her Friends with Her Friends

It's natural to think that weddings are opportune moments to bring your world and your fiancée's world together—in many ways, that's exactly what marriage is all about. But that doesn't mean you should force your guests to sit with a bunch of complete strangers. Put all her college friends at the same table—

they haven't seen each other in years, and they'll have a blast. Put all your coworkers at the same table—it'll make for better stories around the water cooler on Monday morning. If any of your friends want to reach out and meet new people, they'll have no trouble making connections on their own.

Don't Dismiss the Singles Table

The singles table is much maligned in the popular media—what's worse than showing up solo at an event that celebrates togetherness? But anyone who asks this question has clearly never experienced the thrill and elation of a wedding reception hookup. Don't bury your single guests at tables full of married couples or (even worse) new parents. Instead, put them all at a singles table and let the sparks fly.

Your Wedding Is Not a Peace Summit

There may be two people or branches of your family that simply do not get along, or perhaps they have gone years without speaking. If you must invite both parties to your wedding, don't take it upon yourself to be the Great Compromiser. Seat them on opposite sides of the reception and know that they will make peace in the mayhem if they want to.

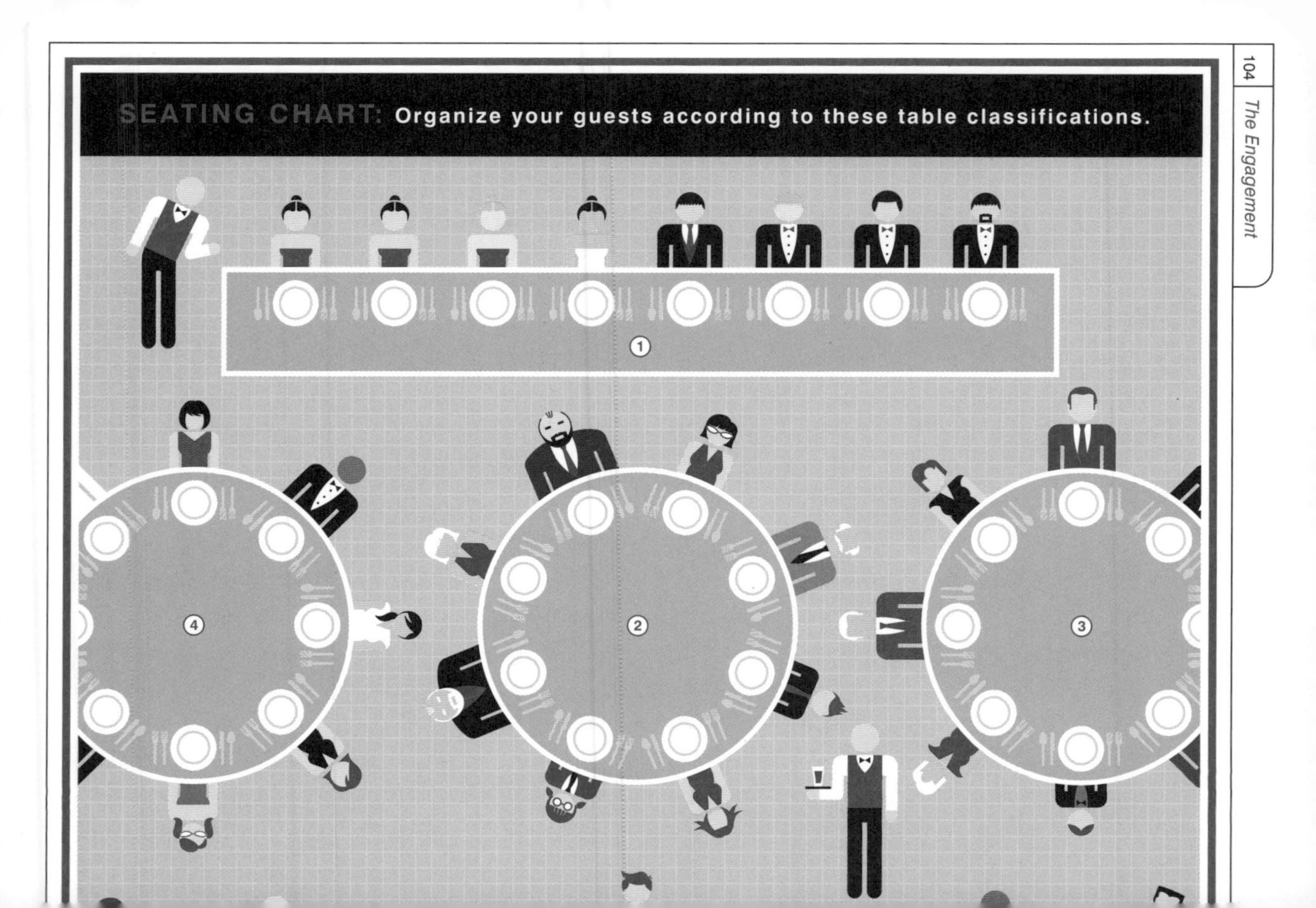
SEATING CHART: Organize your guests according to these table classifications.
1
4
2
3

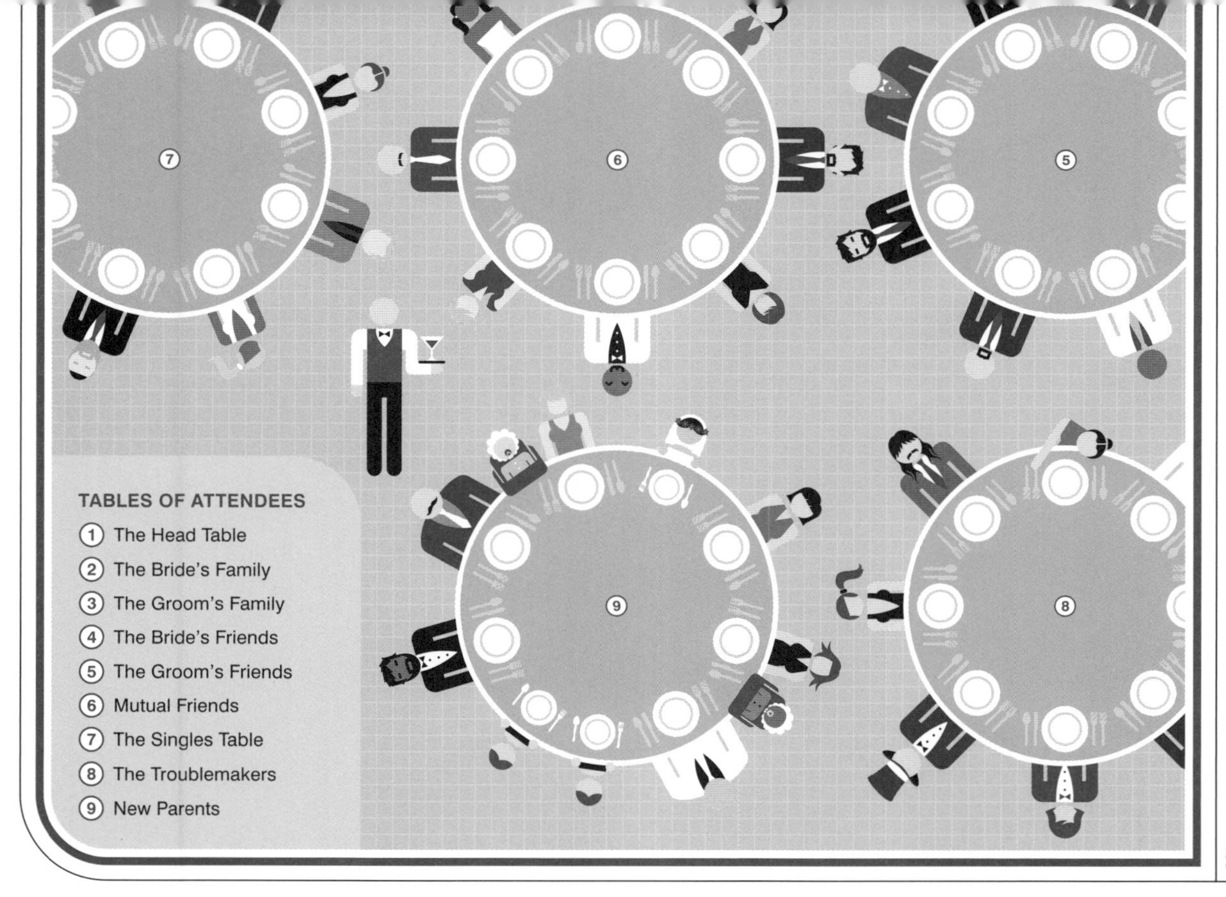

TABLES OF ATTENDEES
1 The Head Table
2 The Bride's Family
3 The Groom's Family
4 The Bride's Friends
5 The Groom's Friends
6 Mutual Friends
7 The Singles Table
8 The Troublemakers
9 New Parents
7
6
5
9
8

Your Uniform and Accessories

You may have seen one of those local news segments about brides-to-be waiting in line for a wedding-gown store to open—and then tearing through the place like elephants let loose on a peanut farm. Just one more example of how women will adopt desperate measures and throw caution to the wind to achieve the most perfect, one-of-a-kind wedding imaginable.

Of course, plenty of grooms stress out over their wedding-day digs. We encourage them to remember this timeless axiom: Nobody is looking at you because everybody is looking at the bride. You are simply an extra who reads his one line—"I do"—and then melts back into the scenery. Granted, you'll want to be the best-dressed scenery ever, but don't fool yourself into believing that anyone but your mother will be laying their eyes on you for more than a few seconds.

Let's Play Dress-Up!

This experience may be so emasculating that it sends you fleeing into permanent hibernation—or it could be like fulfilling the secret James Bond fantasy lifestyle you've bottled up for years. Let's aim for the latter. Here are a few tips to keep you on track.

Be complementary. You certainly want to look dashing, but you don't want to look so stylish that you upstage the bride. Tails are fine if you and your fiancée decide they're fine. If not, then you'll have to save them for your swing-band side project.

Ask the future missus. It's very likely that your fiancée already knows exactly what you'll wear, in which case you can save yourself the trouble and just await her instructions. If not, you won't want to pick any clothing for the wedding without first consulting her, unless you're not that serious about getting married in the first place.

Consider the photo album. You will be inclined, and a tuxedo rental shop may push you, to adopt a current formalwear trend. You can opt for the latest styles if you think they look best, but make your decision with the future in mind. You may think a paisley neon scarf looks tight on your wedding day, but in twenty years your kids will probably find it hysterical.

Consider your surroundings. If you're planning a summer wedding in the South, wearing black tie may land you in the emergency room. These things don't matter as much to your bride because she'll likely have more options for tailoring her attire to fit the weather and the surroundings. Plus, even if she seems to always complain about being too hot or too cold, women are generally tougher than men when high fashion is involved. You'll have fewer options, but definitely consider them all and be prepared to argue if your fiancée is being unreasonable about your uniform—just don't tell her she's being unreasonable.

Consider everyone's budget. Under most circumstances, your groomsmen are expected to cover the costs of their own uniforms. Many may not blink at an outfit that costs several hundred dollars, but others may be on a limited budget. Be thoughtful and remember that your groomsmen may already be spending several hundreds of dollars simply *getting* to your wedding—and they don't end the night with a giant haul of cash and household appliances.

Shop around. One benefit of a black-tie wedding is that you and your groomsmen can simply rent your attire instead of purchasing it. If you don't already have a tailor and/or formalwear provider, shop around for the best deal. And don't lean on your wife. She's got enough to do, and she'll appreciate your taking on this one by yourself—after you've conferred with her on a style choice, natch.

Quality Counts. You won't earn any points for finding the best deal if your tux looks like it's been worn by a barrel jumper in the rodeo. Save money when and where you can, but don't assume that all rented tuxedos look the same. Pay particular attention to frayed cuffs and collars, unraveling seams, stains, and scuffed shoes.

Get to know your tailor. Most of the time, getting fitted for your tuxedo or wedding suit will be much easier than your fiancée's fitting experience. Typically you'll just go to the tuxedo rental place or suit store and have them size you up right there. Either that or you'll just pull your tux or suit out of the closet and make sure it still fits.

However you do it, make sure you do it early. Tailors may take days, weeks, or in extreme cases months to get your suit(s) ready. Don't cut it short—plan on having everything ready 3–6 weeks before your wedding day. And take the lead on making sure your groomsmen do the same.

A Field Guide to Suits

Here is a concise guide to the four most popular choices for today's grooms.

The Penguin Suit

By far the most commonly selected wedding suit style is black tie—a.k.a. the tuxedo in the United States or, simply, a dinner jacket and matching pants in the United Kingdom. Nowadays, this is as formal as most weddings get. Black tie is comprised of:

- Black jacket, either single- or double-breasted and usually limited to one or two buttons, to be closed when wearing lest you want to look like an unsophisticated slob

- Matching black pants, often with a black stripe down the outer seam of both legs

- Bowtie or similar necktie

- White shirt, possibly with disco ruffles but more frequently with vertical pleats or a plain front

- A cummerbund (those fat silk belts) or waistcoat (vest)

- Black patent-leather shoes

From these basics, you are as open to variations as your tailor or local tuxedo rental shop will offer. You can opt for white or silver jacket and pants. You can wear your favorite cufflinks and tiepin. You can have wide ties with Windsor knots, or a puffy scarf like a Latin playboy, or a plaid bowtie and matching waistcoat. You can even opt for tails and a top hat. Just remember that you are an accessory to the bride, so your outfit should always complement (and not overshadow) her own.

The Suit Suit

Your wedding is unlike any other day, so you probably won't want to opt for your average business suit. But if you're on a budget (or just not keen for dressing up like a butler), a blue or charcoal suit can be an excellent option.

It's all in the tie. Sometimes all you need to turn your job-interview suit into your groom's uniform is a great tie. Said accessory will likely be in the wedding's theme color, which might match the bridesmaids' dresses and possibly the flowers or other decorative touches. If you don't know your wedding's theme color, ask your fiancée, because she will definitely know it. And keep an open mind. It may be the furthest thing from your masculine mind to consider anything mauve, but in a wedding context, turning yourself over to some feminine touches might in fact make you look more manly. Also remember that if your groomsmen are dressing in suits, it's customary to purchase ties for them. This is both a nice gesture and a way to avoid any last-minute traumas if any of your groomsmen are less than responsible.

Put quality before economy. If you and your groomsmen are suit-wearing types, you may be able to pull off outfitting everyone without having to buy anything more than the ties. Single-breasted suits can look similar enough, and colors (navy blue, gray, charcoal) are generally close enough, too, so that you may be able just to tell your groomsmen what they need to wear. However, never take for granted that everyone has what he needs. Do whatever you can to confirm that the suits are truly similar enough to pass muster—you don't want to discover an "odd man out" when your groomsmen are standing before the entire congregation.

Let's make a deal. Suit salesmen, like car salesmen, often have some leeway in the prices. It's not something you'll notice when you're buying one suit at a time. But watch what happens to a salesperson's eyes and body language when you tell him or her that you're buying four, six, or even ten suits in one shot. If you work it right, you could get nice suits for you and your groomsmen that will

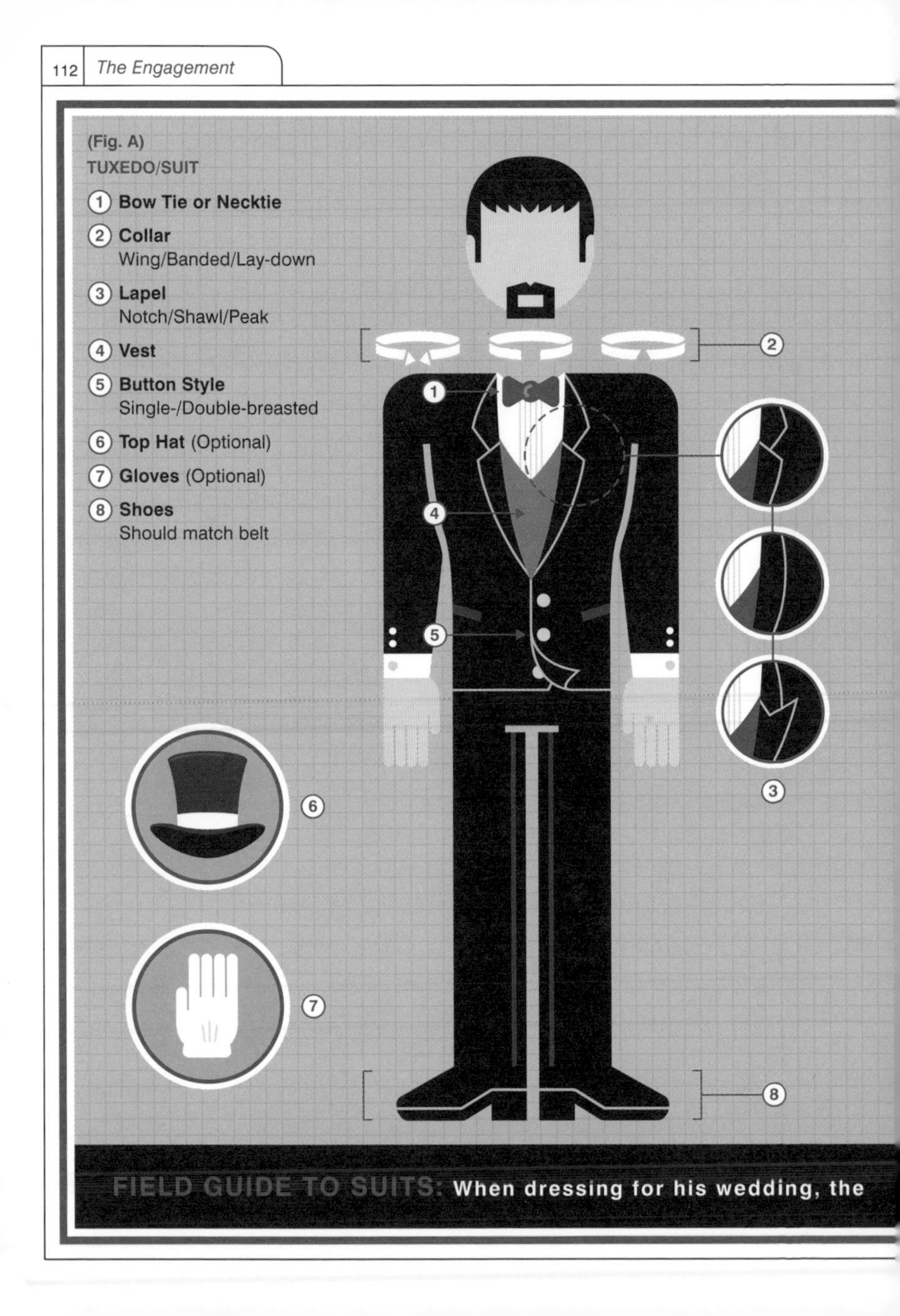

FIELD GUIDE TO SUITS: When dressing for his wedding, the

(Fig. B)
MILITARY SUIT
(Fig. C)
THEME SUIT
modern groom has a variety of options available to him.

have a life beyond your wedding day, often at a price that's less than a tuxedo rental.

Leather goods. If you're going with suits, also remember to tell your groomsmen what accessories and colors will be accepted—usually either black or brown belt and matching shoes.

The Military Suit

This variation doesn't carry the same social baggage as traditional formalwear, mainly because military dress is truly sharp and, in the world of weddings, truly different. If you're a military officer, you've probably already decided on your dress blues and know exactly what you need. If you're not in the military but would like to wear a military outfit, we suggest you call costume shops rather than tuxedo rental places and then hold your reception at Neverland Ranch.

Theme Suits

In the realm of theme weddings, "suits" may not be suits at all but simply outfits that are appropriate to your surroundings. You may get married in all linen on the beach, or you may tie the knot in your Federation finest on the deck of the starship *Enterprise*. The possibilities are too numerous to note in great detail here, but the general rules listed for Suit Suits still apply: (1) Shop around and rent/buy in bulk; (2) don't leave your groomsmen to their own

devices; (3) always consider your surroundings and your budget. Oh, and (4) most important, plan ahead.

Booking the Band (or Other Entertainment)

Contrary to what Adam Sandler may have taught us about choosing a wedding band—or maybe because of what he taught us—selecting the wedding entertainment should be taken quite seriously. Here are some guidelines for picking your dance music:

Match the mood. If the wedding is formal and you're dressed in tails, you'll find a good match with jazz, swing, or even chamber music—but the "Electric Slide" might come off a little tacky. For any other kind of ceremony, the sky's the limit—traditional wedding bands, country-western jugbands, alt-rock DJs, whatever you like. As a general rule, the less formal your wedding, the less formal your music can and should be.

Don't sneer at wedding bands. Sure, they're cheesy. They play the same venues every Friday and Saturday night, spinning "Hot! Hot! Hot!" and "All Night Long" over and over again. But here's the thing: You want the cheese. Nay, you *need* the cheese. Your old college roommate's alt-rock band is no substitute for a professional wedding band. Your reception is not Friday night at the local live music club; it's an artificial event with artificial needs. Wedding bands know this, and they've honed their acts to fit the bill. That doesn't mean you need to pick the cheesiest wedding band you can find—just don't discount them just because of how they make a living.

Don't sneer at cover bands. Those of you who take your music seriously may never, ever consider employing a cover band for your wedding. But you should. Weddings are gatherings of your past, like family and high-school reunions, as much as they're celebrations of your future. Having familiar songs on the soundtrack while you and your bride dance the night away can bring out the memories and help unite a very eclectic guest list (give me a little old lady and a limbo stick, and I'll show you a very happy crowd). Plus, good taste be damned, a wedding just isn't a wedding unless you get a little bit louder now with "Shout!"

Don't sneer at DJs. "If I'm going to have all old songs playing," you might think to yourself, "why not save some cash and pay someone to spin records?" The logic makes sense—but unless your DJ is extremely creative and well established, he won't be able to bring the house down with the same energy as a live band. Plus, good bands who know weddings (see above) are fronted by engaging front men who keep the festivities on track between songs. DJs can also serve this role, but sometimes they're less willing to do so.

Weigh in on the playlist. Most wedding bands make a living by knowing a wide array of "standards"—jazz and pop songs that are familiar and fun. So if you have any special requests that aren't too idiosyncratic, you'll want to quiz your potential bands about them before you do any hiring. Most will tell you to build your own playlist so that they're sure to deliver what you want. If your band balks at that, you might want to consider another choice.

Leave the iPod at home. The beauty of portable music players is that they can hold hours and hours of music that you have personally picked and organized. It's so easy that you may think you can save yourself musical costs altogether and be your own DJ. We advise you to save your body-rockin' for another occasion. For starters, you'll be up the creek if your musical device goes on the fritz. But, more important, this is just one more responsibility you won't want to deal with on your wedding day. If you're on a limited budget (and don't plan to have a lot of dancing at your wedding), consider this option as a last resort, put a responsible friend in charge of it, and make sure you have a second portable music player as a backup.

Musical Playlist Cheat Sheet

Are all of these songs clichés? Yes. Are many of them cheesy? Of course. Are you guaranteed to hear them at 99 percent of weddings? Most definitely. If you're planning anything close to a traditional event, use the following list to identify appropriate songs for different parts of the ceremony and reception. Simply photocopy this list, check off the songs you like, write in additional favorites, and pass it along to your bandleader or DJ. Just remember: The goth tracks that you and your fiancée cherish will probably cause most of your guests to run in terror from the dance floor.

Processional

❑ Arioso by J. S. Bach

❑ Canon in D by Pachelbel

❑ "Romance" (Andante) from Serenade no. 13 for Strings in G major by Mozart

❑ Bridal Chorus ("Here Comes the Bride") from *Lohengrin* by Wagner

❑ Other: ______________________________

Ceremony

❑ Adagio from Sonata in E-flat by Mozart

❑ Air from *Water Music* by Handel

❑ Air on a G String from Orchestral Suite no. 3 by J. S. Bach

❑ Allegro from Brandenburg Concerto no. 4 in G by J. S. Bach

❑ Nocturne in E-flat, op. 9, no. 2, by Chopin

❑ Other: ______________________________

Recessional

❑ "Autumn" (from *The Four Seasons*) by Vivaldi

❑ Traditional Wedding March (from *A Midsummer Night's Dream*) by Mendelssohn

❑ First movement from Brandenburg Concerto no. 1 in F by J. S. Bach

❑ "Alla Hornpipe" (from *Water Music*) by Handel

❑ "Ode to Joy" by Beethoven

❑ Other: ______________________________

Interludes

❑ Air with Variations ("Sheep May Safely Graze") by J. S. Bach

❑ "Amen! Praise and Glory" by Peacock

❑ "Ave Maria" by Schubert

❑ " Finlandia" by Grieg

❑ "Jesu, Joy of Man's Desiring" by J. S. Bach

❑ "The Lord's Prayer"

❑ "O Mio Babbino Caro" (from *Gianna Schicchi*) by Puccini

❑ "Quando Men' Vo" (Musetta's Waltz from *La Bohème*) by Puccini

❑ "Spring" (from *The Four Seasons*) by Vivaldi

❑ Other: ______________________________

First Dance (Husband/Wife)

❑ "A Moment Like This" by Kelly Clarkson

❑ "All I Want Is You" by U2

❑ "At Last" by Etta James

❑ "Because You Loved Me" by Celine Dion

❑ "Can You Feel the Love Tonight" by Elton John

- ❑ "Can't Help Falling in Love" by Elvis Presley
- ❑ "Come Away with Me" by Norah Jones
- ❑ "Could Not Ask for More" by Edwin McCain
- ❑ "End of the Road" by Boys II Men
- ❑ "Endless Love" by Lionel Richie and Diana Ross
- ❑ "(Everything I Do) I Do It for You" by Bryan Adams
- ❑ "How Sweet It Is" by Marvin Gaye
- ❑ "I Fall to Pieces" by Patsy Cline
- ❑ "I Hope You Dance" by Leann Womack
- ❑ "I Will Always Love You" by Dolly Parton or Whitney Houston
- ❑ "Let's Stay Together" by Al Green
- ❑ "More Than Words" by Extreme
- ❑ "Nothing Compares 2 U" by Sinead O'Connor
- ❑ "Thank You" by Dido
- ❑ "Time After Time" by Cyndi Lauper
- ❑ "Unchained Melody" by the Righteous Brothers
- ❑ "When a Man Loves a Woman" by Percy Sledge
- ❑ Other: ________________________________

Father/Daughter

- ❑ "Butterfly Kisses" by Bob Carlisle
- ❑ "Daddy's Hands" by Holly Dunn
- ❑ "Have I Told You Lately" by Rod Stewart
- ❑ "Hero" by Mariah Carey
- ❑ "Isn't She Lovely" by Stevie Wonder
- ❑ "My Girl" by the Temptations

- ❑ "The Way You Look Tonight" by Frank Sinatra
- ❑ Other: ______________________________

Mother/Son

- ❑ "Always" by Atlantic Starr
- ❑ "I Am Your Child" by Barry Manilow
- ❑ "In My Life" by the Beatles
- ❑ "Memories" by Elvis Presley
- ❑ "A Song for Mama" by Boyz II Men
- ❑ "Wind Beneath My Wings" by Bette Middler
- ❑ "You Raise Me Up" by Josh Groban
- ❑ "You've Got a Friend" by James Taylor
- ❑ Other: ______________________________

Jewish Receptions

- ❑ "Hava Nagila"
- ❑ "Mezinka Dance"
- ❑ "Simontov and Mazeltov"
- ❑ "Tzena, Tzena, Tzena"
- ❑ Other: ______________________________

Line Dances (If You Dare)

- ❑ "Achy Breaky Heart" by Billy Ray Cyrus
- ❑ "The Electric Slide" by Marcia Griffiths
- ❑ "The Macarena" by Los Del Rio
- ❑ Other: ______________________________

Crowd-Pleasers

- ❏ "ABC" by the Jackson Five
- ❏ "American Pie" by Don McLean
- ❏ "At Last" by Etta James
- ❏ "Brick House" by the Commodores
- ❏ "Brown-Eyed Girl" by Van Morrison
- ❏ "Celebration" by Kool & the Gang
- ❏ "Dancing Queen" (or anything else) by Abba
- ❏ "Don't Leave Me This Way" by Thelma Houston
- ❏ "I Feel Good" by James Brown
- ❏ "I'll Take You There" by Staple Singers
- ❏ "I'm a Believer" by the Monkees
- ❏ "In the Midnight Hour" by Wilson Pickett
- ❏ "Knock on Wood" by Eddie Floyd
- ❏ "Lady" by Kenny Rogers
- ❏ "Lady Marmalade" by Labelle
- ❏ "Love Shack" by the B-52s
- ❏ "Mony, Mony" by Tommy James and the Shondells
- ❏ "Papa's Got a Brand New Bag" by James Brown
- ❏ "Play That Funky Music" by Wild Cherry
- ❏ "Rapper's Delight" by the Sugar Hill Gang
- ❏ "Respect" by Aretha Franklin
- ❏ "Ring of Fire" by Johnny Cash
- ❏ "Shout" by Otis Day and the Nights
- ❏ "Shout" by the Isley Brothers
- ❏ "Soul Man" by Sam and Dave
- ❏ "Sweet Caroline" by Neil Diamond

- ❑ "Sweet Home Alabama" by Lynyrd Skynrd
- ❑ "This Magic Moment" by the Drifters
- ❑ "The Twist" by Chubby Checker
- ❑ "Twist and Shout" by the Isley Brothers or the Beatles
- ❑ "U Can't Touch This" by MC Hammer
- ❑ "The Way You Look Tonight" by Frank Sinatra
- ❑ "We Are Family" by Sister Sledge
- ❑ "What I Like About You" by the Romantics
- ❑ "Wonderful Tonight" by Eric Clapton
- ❑ "You Sexy Thing" by Hot Chocolate
- ❑ "You've Got a Friend" by Carole King
- ❑ "YMCA" by the Village People
- ❑ Other: ____________________________

Songs to Avoid

- ❑ "Baby Got Back" by Sir Mix-A-Lot
- ❑ "Bitch" by the Rolling Stones
- ❑ "Cry Me a River" by Justin Timberlake
- ❑ "Girls, Girls, Girls" by Mötley Crüe
- ❑ "The Lady Is a Tramp" by Frank Sinatra
- ❑ "Love Is a Battlefield" by Pat Benatar
- ❑ "Pour Some Sugar on Me" by Def Leppard
- ❑ "Super Freak" by Rick James
- ❑ "To All the Girls I've Loved Before" by Willie Nelson and Julio Iglesias
- ❑ "Toxic" by Britney Spears
- ❑ "You're So Vain" by Carly Simon
- ❑ Other: ____________________________

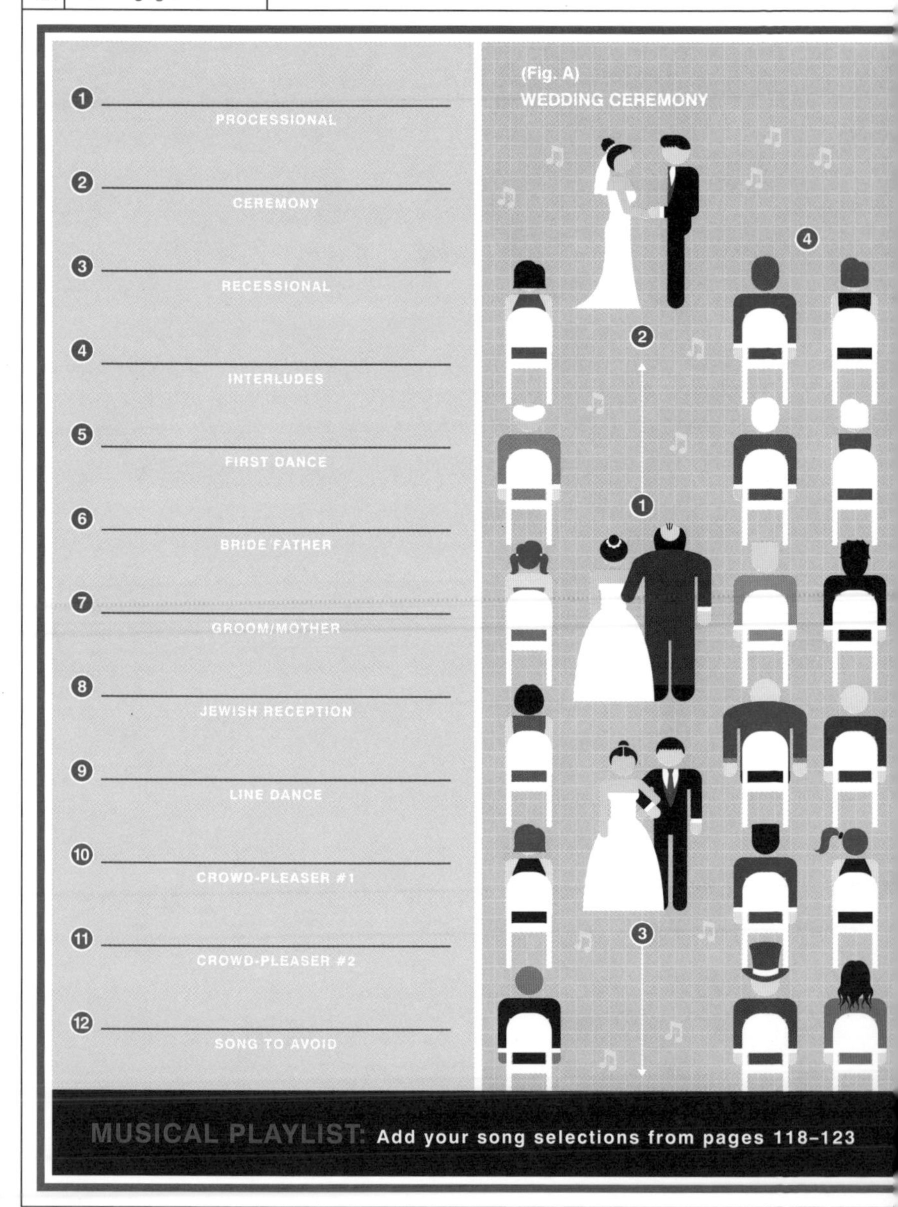

1 PROCESSIONAL
2 CEREMONY
3 RECESSIONAL
4 INTERLUDES
5 FIRST DANCE
6 BRIDE/FATHER
7 GROOM/MOTHER
8 JEWISH RECEPTION
9 LINE DANCE
10 CROWD-PLEASER #1
11 CROWD-PLEASER #2
12 SONG TO AVOID
(Fig. A)
WEDDING CEREMONY
4
2
1
3
MUSICAL PLAYLIST: Add your song selections from pages 118–123

to the corresponding segment of the wedding ceremony or reception.

Hiring a Photographer and/or Videographer

As more and more of us purchase digital cameras and develop interests in digital photography, it's only natural to see that more grooms are taking on the responsibility of finding a good wedding photographer. But just because you dropped $150 on a point-and-shoot Nikon doesn't make you an expert photog. Your wedding will have plenty of unique challenges—if you've ever tried to assemble ten or twenty people for a group photo and make sure all of them have their eyes open, you'll understand what we're talking about. Fortunately, many wedding photographers now showcase their portfolios on personal Web sites, which allow you to sample their work without a personal interview. Once you've limited your candidates to three or four, try to arrange face-to-face meetings and keep the following considerations in mind.

This Ain't the Amateur Hour

Perhaps your cousin is a college student majoring in photography, and she's offered to save you some cash. Encourage her to take as many photos as she likes—but go ahead and hire a professional photographer, anyway. You're better off with someone who's made a career of capturing weddings on film (and memory cards). Professionals can set up and break down with the least bit of distraction, and they've been to enough weddings to know all the standard cues.

Ask About Equipment

When meeting with photographers, ask what kind of equipment they use, because they're going to need more than a built-in flash and auto zoom. If your photographer is a good one, he or she should ask questions about the type of ceremony you're planning to anticipate any special equipment needs.

Own Your Wedding

Back when photography was primarily a film-based medium, most wedding photographers would hang onto the negatives, and they would make any reprints (often at a steep price) if you needed them. But with the advent of digital cameras and print-at-home technology, there's no reason why you shouldn't receive all your wedding photographs on a disk or memory card so that you can print and frame to your heart's content. Your photographer may want to retain reprint rights for a portfolio or other needs, and that's fine. But be sure that your contract specifies that you own the images.

Employ Viral Photography

Your official photographer will take hundreds of lovely, well-composed shots that your grandmother and grandfather will fawn over. But who will photograph the Best Man drinking from his flask in the moments before his toast? Or the two bridesmaids who shocked everyone by making out on the dance floor? These are

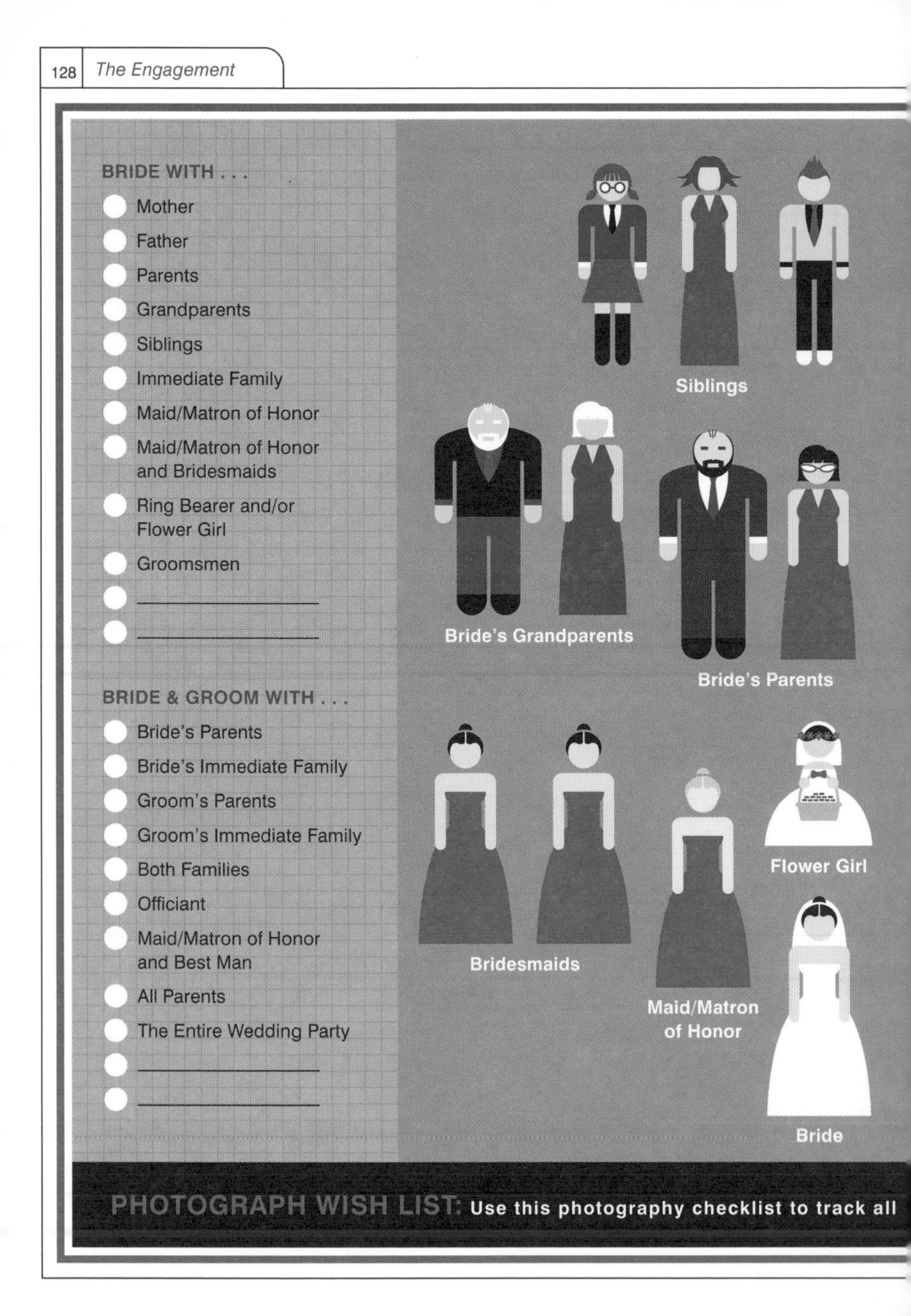

BRIDE WITH . . .
Mother
Father
Parents
Grandparents
Siblings
Immediate Family
Maid/Matron of Honor
Maid/Matron of Honor and Bridesmaids
Ring Bearer and/or Flower Girl
Groomsmen
BRIDE & GROOM WITH . . .
Bride's Parents
Bride's Immediate Family
Groom's Parents
Groom's Immediate Family
Both Families
Officiant
Maid/Matron of Honor and Best Man
All Parents
The Entire Wedding Party
Siblings
Bride's Grandparents
Bride's Parents
Flower Girl
Bridesmaids
Maid/Matron of Honor
Bride
PHOTOGRAPH WISH LIST: Use this photography checklist to track all

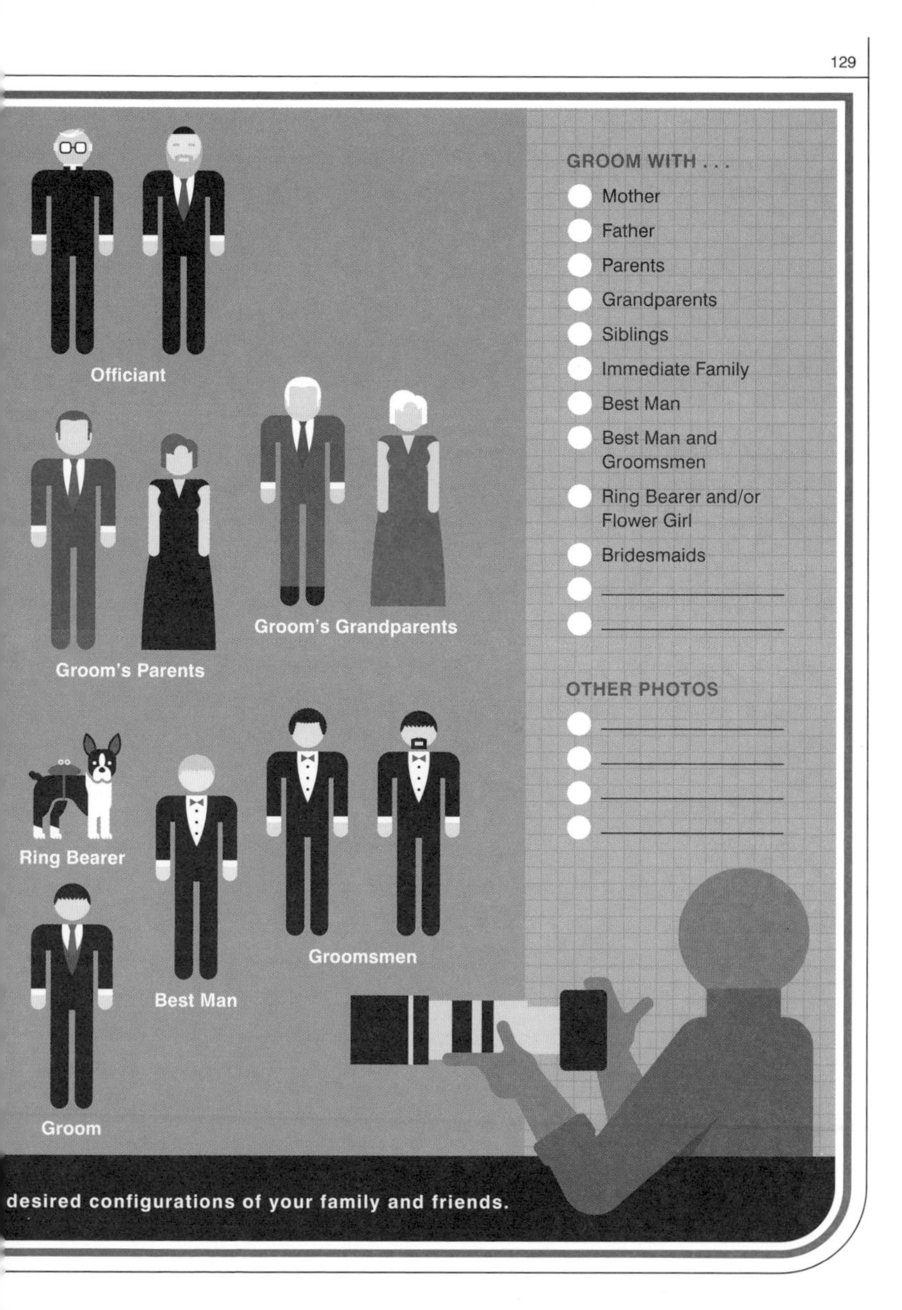
Officiant
Groom's Parents
Groom's Grandparents
Ring Bearer
Best Man
Groomsmen
Groom
GROOM WITH . . .
Mother
Father
Parents
Grandparents
Siblings
Immediate Family
Best Man
Best Man and Groomsmen
Ring Bearer and/or Flower Girl
Bridesmaids
OTHER PHOTOS
desired configurations of your family and friends.

moments you definitely want to capture on film—especially those bridesmaids—and there is a simple and inexpensive solution: Buy a handful of instant cameras and place them at the reception (one per table if people are sitting down). Then create a drop-off box where people can leave the cameras at the end of the event. Also, since many of your guests will probably bring their own cameras, request that people e-mail their best pictures directly to you.

And If You're Videotaping . . .

Most of what applies to a good photographer applies to a good videographer, if you choose to hire one. We'll provide just one

additional piece of advice: Manage your expectations. There's a wide gulf between Martin Scorsese and the guy who shoots your wedding. Expect kooky screen wipes, goofy music, and an end product that is both remarkably cheesy and incredibly fun to watch. If there's such a thing as a classy and sophisticated wedding video, we have yet to see it.

The One Word No Fiancée Wants to Hear . . .

Prenup. Whenever you read a news story about a prenuptial agreement, it usually involves a celebrity and/or an extremely wealthy person. That's good news for the rest of us. If you're not a celebrity and not extremely wealthy, you probably don't need a prenuptial agreement. Nevertheless, it can't hurt to understand how they work and why you might consider getting one anyway.

What Is a Prenup?

A prenuptial agreement is a signed proclamation of what should happen to your and your wife's assets and liabilities in the event of divorce or death. All states provide some form of legal precedent for how these issues are handled in both cases; the prenup is meant to override these precedents.

DO I NEED A PRENUP?

◯ Yes ◯ No	**Do I have a personal or family fortune or other assets (art collections, real estate holdings, etc.) that I need to protect?**
◯ Yes ◯ No	**Do I have other beneficiaries (that is, children from a previous marriage, ailing parents) who need guaranteed protection of rights to my assets in case of my death or incapacitation?**
◯ Yes ◯ No	**Do I have a history of debt from which I would like to protect my wife?**
◯ Yes ◯ No	**Does your employer require you to have one? (This becomes an issue when companies offer partial ownership of a firm to a particular employee.)**
◯ Yes ◯ No	**Do I have reason not to give to my wife the power of attorney over my personal, business, and medical affairs if I should become incapacitated or die?**

⚠ ***CAUTION:*** *If you've answered "no" to all the above questions, then you probably don't need a prenup and your fiancée will think that you're a creep for requesting one. Of course, pragmatists will point out that 50 percent of marriages end in divorce, which means there's a 50/50 chance that your partnership with your wife will eventually dissolve. In these cases, a solid prenup can spare hours of stressful arguments, not to mention thousands of dollars in legal fees.*

How Do I Ask My Fiancée to Sign a Prenup?

Very, very, carefully. If your fiancée has a background in business or law, you might remind her that starting a marriage is very much like starting a small business, complete with special laws, tax exemptions, joint accounting, shared expenses, and so on. Using this analogy, the prenup is simply a legally binding exit strategy in the event that the business tanks.

If your fiancée has a background in art, poetry, drama, or virtually anything else, you're out of luck. Your fiancée has watched far too many Meg Ryan/Sandra Bullock/Julia Roberts movies in which the bad guys are always asking for prenups. To date, there are no known effective ways of asking for a prenup without sounding like a jerk—so make sure it's really important to you.

How Do I Get One?

This is relatively easy—but it sure ain't cheap. You need to seek legal counsel. You and your wife will need to hire separate attorneys. Both should be involved in the drafting of the prenup. Both should be present at the signing of the prenup. Otherwise, it may not be upheld in court.

By the way, be prepared for "full and fair disclosure"—all of your assets, income, liabilities, and even expectancies (anything you may stand to gain in the foreseeable future, such as an inheritance) must be detailed before the prenup is drafted. Anything hidden will complicate matters and may deem the prenup null and void.

A Million Little Pieces

By this point you're probably getting tired of being told how to behave. We feel for you, brother, even if this book is doing all the telling. What makes wedding planning so daunting for so many guys is that so much of the work is strictly hypothetical—up until the final hours, there is precious little for you to lift, move, carry, or simply ***do***.

Except, of course, for the following chores: all actual, honest-to-goodness tasks that you can perform with your bare hands.

Buy the Wedding Rings

This should sound like music to your ears: Wedding bands are generally cheaper than engagement rings, and your fiancée gets to select the one she's going to wear. Those two factors can make all the difference.

Plus, you get a ring this time, too. Your fiancée may wish to make a symbolic gesture by picking out your wedding band, but we suggest that you talk her out of this. She's got enough on her plate, and you'll do the work more efficiently. Be sure to purchase the rings well in advance; the most important inanimate object at the wedding is the hardware in your best man's pocket, so buy it well before (six weeks minimum) the big day.

Finally, make sure the rings fit before you are both standing in front of the officiant, your personal deity, and all your friends and family. Wedding Bloat is a real phenomenon in which the stress of planning a reception causes the groom (but rarely the bride) to pack on a few pounds. Even if your rings fit in the store, there's no guarantee they'll fit when it matters. Take five seconds the week before the ceremony and make sure they're right.

Complete a Gift Registry

Just like your birthday, your wedding is the rare opportunity to receive gifts without any obligation of giving gifts in return (until, of course, your buddies start planning weddings of their own). But before you get too carried away and start registering for all manner of video game systems and plasma televisions, be aware that the vast majority of wedding presents are utterly impractical and boring—we're talking china, silver, crystal, linens, and other things that will go on the top shelf in the closet you never open,

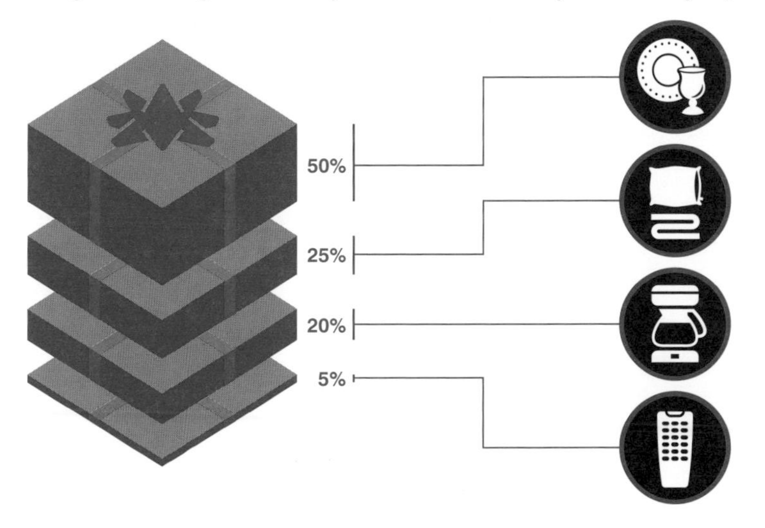

driving up your home insurance while they gather dust.

Of course, these gifts do have their benefits. China and silver are certainly solid investments—they could be family heirlooms that you one day pass on to a son or daughter. Alternatively, they could be sold for major money at estate sales or as part of divorce proceedings. The point is, they won't lose value like the TV sets or video game consoles you've been eyeballing.

In the end, of course, you're bound to end up with a few choice toys, all courtesy of your oldest and closest friends—your groomsmen. If these guys give you water goblets, we advise you to reconsider these friendships.

Obtain a Marriage License

Even if the pope himself officiates your wedding, you won't be married in the eyes of the law without an official document from your city, state, or country of residence. Most officiants can advise you what to do, and a few may even provide the license for you. But never take for granted that this responsibility is anyone's but your own. Bring the paperwork to the rehearsal or the wedding ceremony, depending on your plans (the best way to know is to ask your officiant). Then make sure you sign the document after you say your vows on the wedding day, otherwise your kiss won't stick.

Different cities and states have different laws, and it is beyond the scope of this book to describe exactly what needs to be done in every situation. But there is one generalization that applies to anyone seeking a marriage license: The process is more complicated, more time-consuming, and even more expensive than you expect. The wheels of government bureaucracy turn slowly, so investigate the procedure at least 90 days before the wedding. Keep your checkbook handy, along with multiple forms of identification. And don't be surprised if you need to provide a blood sample.

Attend a Caterer's "Tasting"

Don't let your fiancée cheat you out of this "responsibility," because you have every bit as much a right to a delicious free

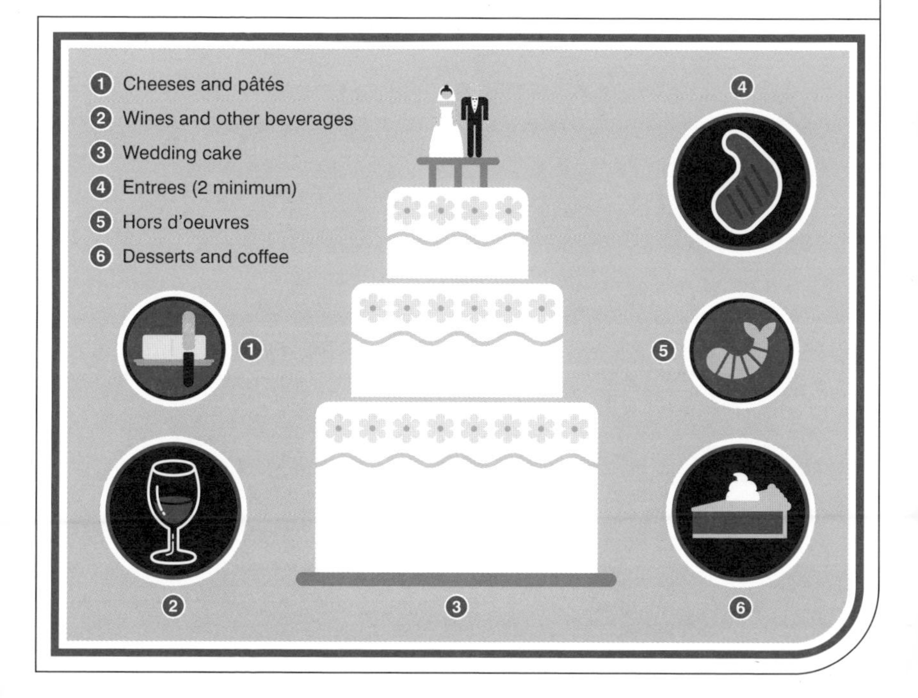

meal as she does. That's right—most caterers will include a complimentary "tasting" as part of their package, in which you, your bride, and often several of your most trusted advisors can sample everything on the menu to determine which foods will be most appropriate for your reception. Among the many decisions made will be the best choice of a wedding cake, so plan to attend.

Part of this experience may also include the "groom's cake," which is a smaller cake, typically chocolate, that is also cut at the reception. Not all people choose to serve them, but if nothing else they provide an apt metaphor for the wedding in general: The "wedding cake" is really the bride's cake, and you get the other dinky cake on the side. Embrace it.

Practice Your Dance Moves

If you're going to have music at your wedding, you will likely be expected to have a "first dance" with your new wife. For some of us, not a problem. If you've got the right moves, you'll know it—we just recommend that you spend fifteen minutes ahead of time practicing with your fiancée. But if you find the idea of dancing in front of an audience to be absolutely terrifying, you might think about investing in dance lessons. They will certainly ease the wedding-day jitters, provide some useful skills that will aid you at social functions to come, and help keep the emphasis on romance during your engagement.

Choosing Floral Arrangements

Why are you reading this? Most men with any common sense have already skipped ahead to the next section. You should not be choosing the flowers for your wedding. We bet you probably can't even name five different flowers. Go ahead. Prove us wrong.

If your fiancée is badgering you to play a role in meeting with florists, do yourself a favor. Underline the following sentence and stick it under your fiancée's nose: A man should play no role in selecting the flowers for his wedding.

Purchase the Zero Anniversary Gift

Your wedding is the beginning of something pretty dang significant, so you should start off right by getting your bride a gift worthy of the occasion. What's "worthy" will vary widely from woman to woman, but suffice to say that this occasion is not a normal one, and any kind of normal gift will not do. Jewelry is generally a good option (even though you've already sprung for an engagement ring and a wedding band). But you can save money by being creative. If your wife has a favorite book, find an autographed first edition on the Internet. Or put together a photo album of all your favorite memories. The gift doesn't need to be expensive; it just needs to look like you put some thought into it. Jump on this task early, especially if it takes extra effort on your part, because you will be much too busy in the final weeks for extensive crafting or shopping.

Purchase Gifts for Your Groomsmen

You are obliged, though not strictly required, to give your groomsmen a token of your appreciation. This token can be as fancy or as inconsequential as you like. If you're Daddy Warbucks, give them all season tickets to the Yankees. If you're thrifty, get them all pocketknives. Our only suggestion is that you don't give anything that feels too much like a corporate tchotchke. A quality laptop carrying bag with your wedding date embroidered on it ain't cool—but a quality laptop carrying bag, for the right groomsman, could be perfect.

Purchase Party Favors

While tchotchkes make poor gifts for your groomsmen, the rest of your wedding guests might enjoy them. If your budget permits, think about giving away some kind of inconsequential memento at the wedding reception. Some suggestions that seem to go over well include mugs, CDs featuring your wedding songs, beer cozies with your wedding date, and the ever-popular snow globes with bride-and-groom inside. With the explosion of new retailers on the Internet, ever-more-creative choices are available if you're willing to dig around.

Settle Things with God

Caterers, photographers, and wedding bands will all expect some kind of deposit before providing services, but most churches or synagogues will not. Nevertheless, it is a good practice to make a donation to the venue on behalf of the engaged couple. This is traditionally the groom's responsibility. The amount of the donation can vary widely, and the chatty secretary in your church's office might be just the right person to ask. Alternatively, ask your parents, your friends, or your wedding planner about what others have done in similar situations.

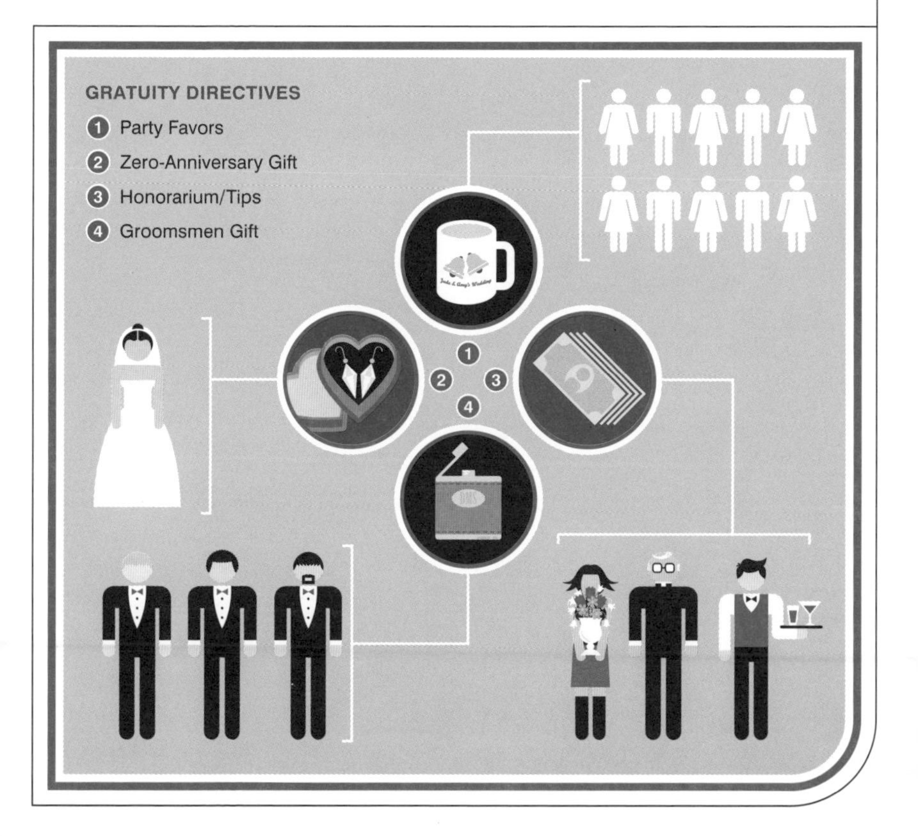

Get Your Tips Together

Most of the people you deal with at the wedding will build all their fees right into their contracts. Some might charge you less, with the implicit understanding that if you enjoy their services, you will tip them. Since weddings can frequently be self-contained events—and you'll want to have this task out of the way as soon as possible—try to take care of tips on the wedding day or before, and don't be shy to pay in cash and throw around the Benjamins (or maybe just the Hamiltons) like you're a gangsta. Just keep in mind that you should only consider yourself responsible for tips to the people whose overall services fall under your budget. Anything being covered by parents or another third party will be handled by them all the way through, unless they tell you otherwise.

Basic Relationship Maintenance

Whether your wedding is large or small, you're bound to reach a point where you feel less like you're planning a momentous occasion based on the love of a lifetime and more like you've gone into business with a friend on a venture that can't possibly end in profit. This is normal. Thankfully, a handful of remedies built right into the engagement process will help ease this stressful time.

Getting Schooled

Most people consider couples counseling to be for serious conflicts only. Yet, as you've probably read in just about every self-help screed ever published, the best way to solve problems is to head them off before they become problems. During an engagement, that means understanding what's behind the feeling that you're meant for each other.

If you're getting married under the auspices of your religious faith, said faith may require some level of counseling—either alone with the officiant or in a larger class filled with couples preparing for marriage. Whatever you do, it'll likely be elementary and may occasionally seem quite bizarre, but you're well advised to take the process seriously. Not only will it give you insight into your relationship (How do you achieve balance as a couple? What do you expect from marriage?), but it may also give you more talking points the next time somebody asks you what you like so much about your fiancée.

If you plan a secular marriage, or if your faith doesn't require any special counseling, you can likely still find local professionals who will see you and your fiancée for a nominal fee. If you feel like you're flying blind into impending marriage, this cash outlay could be money well spent.

Of course, if everything's just peachy, don't force the issue. Some people need counseling and know it. Some people don't think they need counseling but do. And some people just don't need it.

Keep the Romance Alive

When you're planning an event for one hundred guests or more, it's easy to lose track of the "little things"—including the very precious love that brought you and your fiancée together. During the engagement, we recommend that you go out of your way to remind your fiancée of the passion and deep feelings that first sparked your romance.

Of course, if you're the kind of guy who's uncomfortable with words like "passion," "romance," and "deep feelings," we can talk in more practical terms: You may reach a point in your engagement when your fiancée is so stressed out that she no longer wants to have sex. If that occurs, we recommend you go out of your way to remind her of the passion and deep feelings that led to your first sexual encounter. Here's how:

- **Go on dates.** Spend some quality time alone together before you have a house full of kids. Dinner and a movie, a picnic in the park, surprise skydiving lessons, even take-out Chinese food with a movie rental can fit the bill nicely. Make a promise to each other that you will not discuss the wedding for the duration of the evening.

- **Go out with friends.** If you and your fiancée have been grappling with some pretty tough decisions mano a mano, blow off some steam with a gang of your closest friends.

- **Give her massages.** She's stressed out. You have strong hands. It's really not that hard.

■ **Give her a day at the spa.** She's stressed out. You have weak hands but a strong credit card. It's really not that hard.

■ **Buy her flowers.** Almost all women like getting flowers, especially when there's no particular occasion, so order or pick some up and surprise her.

⚠ ***Caution:*** *Steer clear of giving chocolates during engagements because your fiancée may be on a life-sucking wedding-gown diet.*

■ **Consider dance classes.** This idea was suggested earlier in the book, but it's so good it bears repeating. Dance lessons will get you in peak condition for the all-important "first dance" at your reception, and it's impossible to go home from these classes without getting a little action.

Write Your Own Marriage Vows

Most people will opt to follow the traditional vows (to have and to hold, for better or worse, 'til death do you part). But if you're looking to fan the flames of passion, few activities are less effective than drafting wedding vows straight from the heart. If you and your fiancée want to try it, follow these guidelines.

■ **Establish ground rules.** Discuss what the vows should be with your fiancée and/or your officiant.

■ **Focus on your fiancée's most positive qualities.** Trust us: Zingers like "I promise never to complain about your cooking" will not

I, [YOUR FULL NAME], take you, [BRIDE'S FULL NAME]

(A) to be my wife.

(B) to be my love, my companion, my rock, and my wife.

(C) to be my number one pal.

(D) to be the Yoko to my John.

(E) to take this journey with me.

You

(A) amaze me with your compassion and beauty.

(B) enchant me with your smile, thrill me with your energy, warm me with your compassion.

(C) are the most wonderful person I've ever met and I can't live without you.

(D) come from more money than I do, which makes your decision to marry me all the more astonishing.

(E) seem like you'd be great in the sack, but of course this hypothesis has yet to be proven.

I promise to

(A) love and cherish you for the rest of our lives.

(B) be your rock and your compass, as you will be mine.

(C) devote myself only to you.

(D) not embarrass you in front of your friends and coworkers.

(E) support you financially because your degree in ______ is worthless in today's job market.

Together, we can

(A) share our joy and love with each other from this day forward.

(B) live and grow and love.

(C) form a bond that can never be broken.

(D) discover the monotony of a long-term monogamous relationship.

(E) double our net worth and become eligible for greater tax breaks.

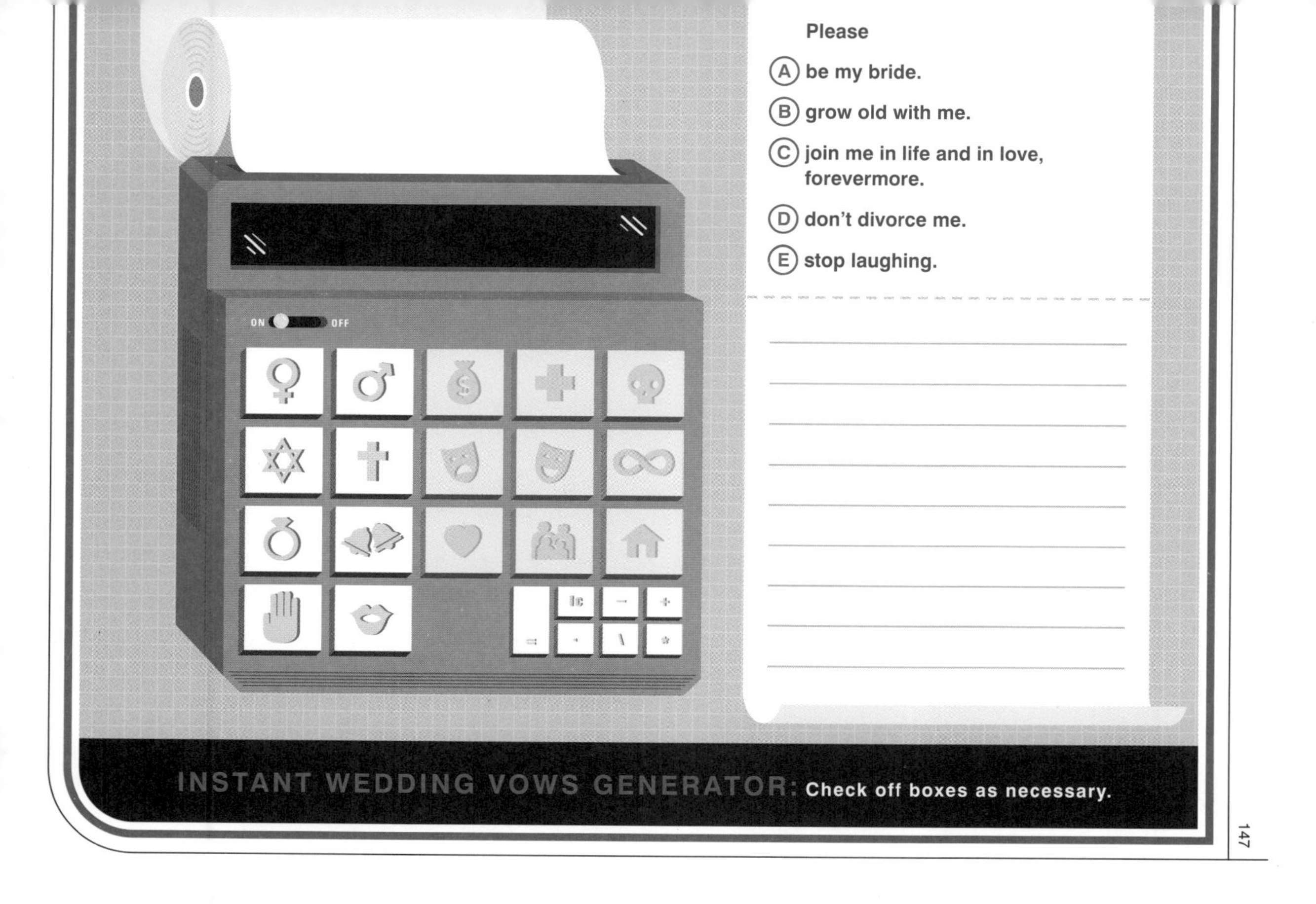
ON
OFF
Please
(A) be my bride.
(B) grow old with me.
(C) join me in life and in love, forevermore.
(D) don't divorce me.
(E) stop laughing.
INSTANT WEDDING VOWS GENERATOR: Check off boxes as necessary.

evoke riotous laughter when you're standing before an entire congregation. You'll just sound like a dick.

■ **Write them down.** Even if you're a state debate champion, you'll never know how stressful it can be to stand at the altar (or under a *huppah*) with the rest of your life on the line. You may be convinced you have your vows memorized, but keep a hard copy in the inside pocket of your wedding jacket, just in case.

■ **Practice.** You'll be speaking the vows to your bride, but dozens or hundreds of guests will be listening right along with her. In fact, your officiant may even hold a microphone to your lips, amplifying the vows for the entire audience—so now is not the time to be stammering. By preparing in advance—and reciting your vows at least a dozen times—you won't find yourself tongue-tied on your wedding day.

Planning the Honeymoon

One of the more traditional groom responsibilities is making arrangements for the honeymoon. At the risk of being repetitious, we must urge you (again) to consult your fiancée. Nothing will spoil a fairy-tale wedding faster than a honeymoon that's only good for half of the honeymooners.

The Practical Planner

Even if you've traveled to more cities than USAir, you've probably never experienced a trip quite like a honeymoon. This is not just another 7- or 10-day vacation. Keep these pointers in mind:

■ **Consult friends, family, and the Internet.** You may not want to copy somebody else's honeymoon exactly, but you can certainly look to others for inspiration. Then hit up your old friend the Web and see which lovely locale is cheapest and/or most practical for the dates you'll be traveling.

■ **No surprises.** Unless your track record with your fiancée is flawless, don't try your luck on the honeymoon. A weeklong surprise that isn't received well on day one will make days two through whenever downright miserable.

■ **Know what you want.** And by that we really mean "know what your fiancée wants." You may have grand plans for a golf vacation or an outdoor adventure, but if the brand-new missus isn't down with that, you are heading for disaster.

■ **Don't invite anyone else.** This should be obvious, but to a surprising number of people, it's not. Your honeymoon is for you and your fiancée, period. Solitude is the reward you get for making it through the engagement and wedding, so don't mess it up by thinking that a double-dating

Planning the Honeymoon
Factors to consider when planning your honeymoon
extravagance of accommodations, all-inclusive food

LODGING INFORMATION

MR.	First Name	Initial	Last Name
MRS.	First Name	Initial	Last Name

Hotel/Resort	Room/Suite #
Address (Number and Street)	City

State/Province	Country	Zip/Postal Code

DATE ☐☐ / ☐☐ / ☐☐ through ☐☐ / ☐☐ / ☐☐

DAYS ☐☐ x RATE ☐☐☐☐.☐☐ = TOTAL ☐☐☐☐☐.☐☐

Bed Size	○ King	○ CA King
Butler Service	○ Yes	○ No
All-Inclusive	○ Yes	○ No

TRANSPORTATION

○ ○ ○

○ ○

include geographic location and climate, activity endurance level, and drink, duration of trip, and, of course, budgetary limitations.

ACTIVITIES

	ROMANCE	ADVENTURE	FITNESS	FUN & SUN
SEDENTARY	 ○	 ○	 ○	 ○
ACTIVE	 ○	 ○	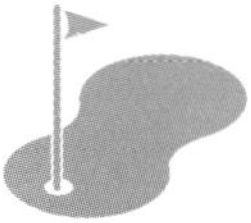 ○	 ○
VERY ACTIVE	 ○	 ○	 ○	 ○
EXTREME	 ○	 ○	 ○	 ○

trip or—heaven forbid—family-vacation-slash-honeymoon can yield the same benefits, unless your goal is a quick annulment.

■ **Know your maximum.** Some people can lie on a beach until retirement. Others get antsy after four days. Know how long you and your wife can survive in each other's company and away from it all. Many honeymooners enjoy a trip that shifts gears halfway through—three to five days on a lounge chair to recover from the shock of the wedding, followed by three to five days of more demanding and adventurous travel.

■ **Know your minimum.** On the flipside, don't be so brief that you barely have time to take off your shoes. Weddings are crowded, loud, traumatic events, and you'll want some time before you have to get back to reality. Three days is usually a good minimum—longer than a weekend, shorter than can cause problems if real life is anxiously awaiting your return.

■ **Embrace the cliché.** You may have an irresistible urge to avoid other newlyweds on your honeymoon, and perhaps that's why you're ruling out tropical islands and mountain getaways. But before you buy two round-trip tickets to Manhattan (or London or Paris), just remember that your wedding is a big, chaotic event, and you might not wish to follow it up by visiting a big, chaotic city. Even the most stubborn urban adventurers can become fond of sand and sun when confronting a serious case of post-wedding exhaustion.

■ **Know your adventure threshold.** Perhaps you read that last tip and you're still not convinced. That's fine—you're perfectly within your rights to prove that the dream honeymoon can also be the dream vacation. Still, do everything you can to cut down on flight times and ratchet up the creature comforts, even if it means spending a little extra. You'll appreciate that you did.

■ **Know your spending limit.** As with everything else for this damned event, the honeymoon is going to set you back some scratch, so figure out what you have to spend and plan accordingly. You may have to choose between having a short but luxurious vacation or a longer one with half the amenities. On one hand, you can't miss what you haven't experienced, so having half the extravagances may be just fine. On the other hand, you may never again get a chance to go all out, so it might do you right (and earn you years of goodwill with your wife) to opt for opulence. If you can afford both, bring us along, please.

■ **Make sure people know you're on a honeymoon.** Many hotels and resorts exist to service honeymooners. So as you're making reservations, don't be shy about telling people it's for your honeymoon. Some may provide chilled champagne, upgraded accommodations, or simply fresh flowers. These amenities can be a nice reminder that this vacation is unlike any other.

■ **Do something, do anything.** If you're thinking of postponing the honeymoon, you still must make plans to get away for a few days immediately after the wedding. A family cabin, a bed-and-breakfast, a motel with a pool that's ten miles from your house—whatever it is, go there and get acquainted with your new life companion. Otherwise your life might not feel different enough post-nuptials to have justified all the activity.

Planning the Rehearsal Dinner

The rehearsal dinner is typically a small-scale gathering on the night before the wedding, often (as the name implies) immediately after a rehearsal of the ceremony. The guest list usually consists of participants in the ceremony—your most immediate family, your closest friends, and all members of the wedding party.

Not every wedding has a rehearsal dinner (a lot of smaller ones skip it). But if you do have one, it will traditionally be up to you and your family to plan and pay for it.

A Family Affair

In addition to being a great kickoff to a full-blown wedding weekend, rehearsal dinners are also the perfect plaything for your mother. You'll recall from pages 70–71 that your mother is the highest-ranking woman in the wedding whose participation is optional. But you'll also remember that if she suspects that's the

case, you'll have more than one woman to keep calm throughout the engagement.

Which is where the rehearsal dinner comes into play. Here's an event your mother can truly immerse herself in. We recommend that you let her run a long leash—twenty years from now, your fondest memories will be of the wedding itself, not the rehearsal dinner, so there's no point in stressing out over this event.

Nevertheless, you (and your fiancée) may want to chime in about several key negotiation points:

How fancy should it be? For many couples, the rehearsal dinner is typically one degree less formal than the wedding itself. If you are planning a grandiose wedding, the rehearsal dinner will be semiformal. If you're planning a semiformal wedding, the rehearsal dinner will be casual. If you're planning a casual wedding, the rehearsal dinner will be a toga party. But no hard and fast rules define this event. Look at your budget, figure out how much you (and/or your parents) want to spend, and then plan accordingly.

Who gets to come? Your mother may mistakenly believe that since she is planning the rehearsal dinner, she can make the guest list. She's only half right. As the matriarch of your side of the family, she definitely gets a vote. But you must balance her whims with your own desires and those of your fiancée's family. If you cannot include all the following people, you might rethink the dinner with a more modest budget:

- **The Wedding Party.** You'll want to include all your groomsmen and bridesmaids; if they don't know one another, this is a great way for them to get acquainted. Consult with the parents of flower girls, ring bearers, and other young children in the wedding party; if the dinner conflicts with an early bedtime, you should feel free to leave them off the guest list.

- **Family.** Any family members with roles in the wedding ceremony should be invited, and in most circumstances you will want all your parents and siblings there, too.

- **Close Friends.** Any other people with roles in the wedding (readers, ushers, and the like) should be invited to the rehearsal dinner. And if your parents have any close friends who are "like family," you may invite them as well.

Are toasts involved? It's a given that your best man will give some kind of toast at your wedding reception, but the rehearsal dinner allows other friends and family members the chance to make toasts of their own. Decide if you want them to do so, consult with your fiancée, and then make your wishes known. Of course, if you shy away from the spotlight, don't be surprised if your friends ignore your wishes and tell your embarrassing spring-break story, anyway. We suggest you roll with the punches and ask your fiancée to do the same. Friends will be friends, and even if their toasts are mortifying, they are almost certainly making them out of admiration for you and your bride-to-be. So let them have their moment and continue to enjoy your own.

What about you? If you don't plan to write your own vows, then the rehearsal dinner is the most appropriate moment to publicly express your love of and devotion to your fiancée in your own words. We're not saying you should feel obliged to do so. But after the trauma of the engagement and before the insanity of the wedding day, a few loving words, recited in front of your closest family and friends, could calm your nerves, make you look like a hero, and remind your fiancée why she said "yes" in the first place.

Surviving Your Bachelor Party

Here it is, your true reward for many long months of economic and personal hardship: a night to end all nights, spent with your boys. You will get dangerously intoxicated. Women wearing clothes affixed solely with adhesive will cozy up on your lap or throw you over theirs. You'll eat a steak so large and so raw that it still qualifies as livestock. It'll be a night to remember specifically because you won't remember much of it.

At least that's the conventional wisdom on bachelor parties, passed down from father to son for millennia. Your own final celebration without your fiancée may include all those traditions and more, or it may include none at all. The real yardstick isn't how much you can get away with, it's how much you can do exactly what you want to do. Here are some general guidelines.

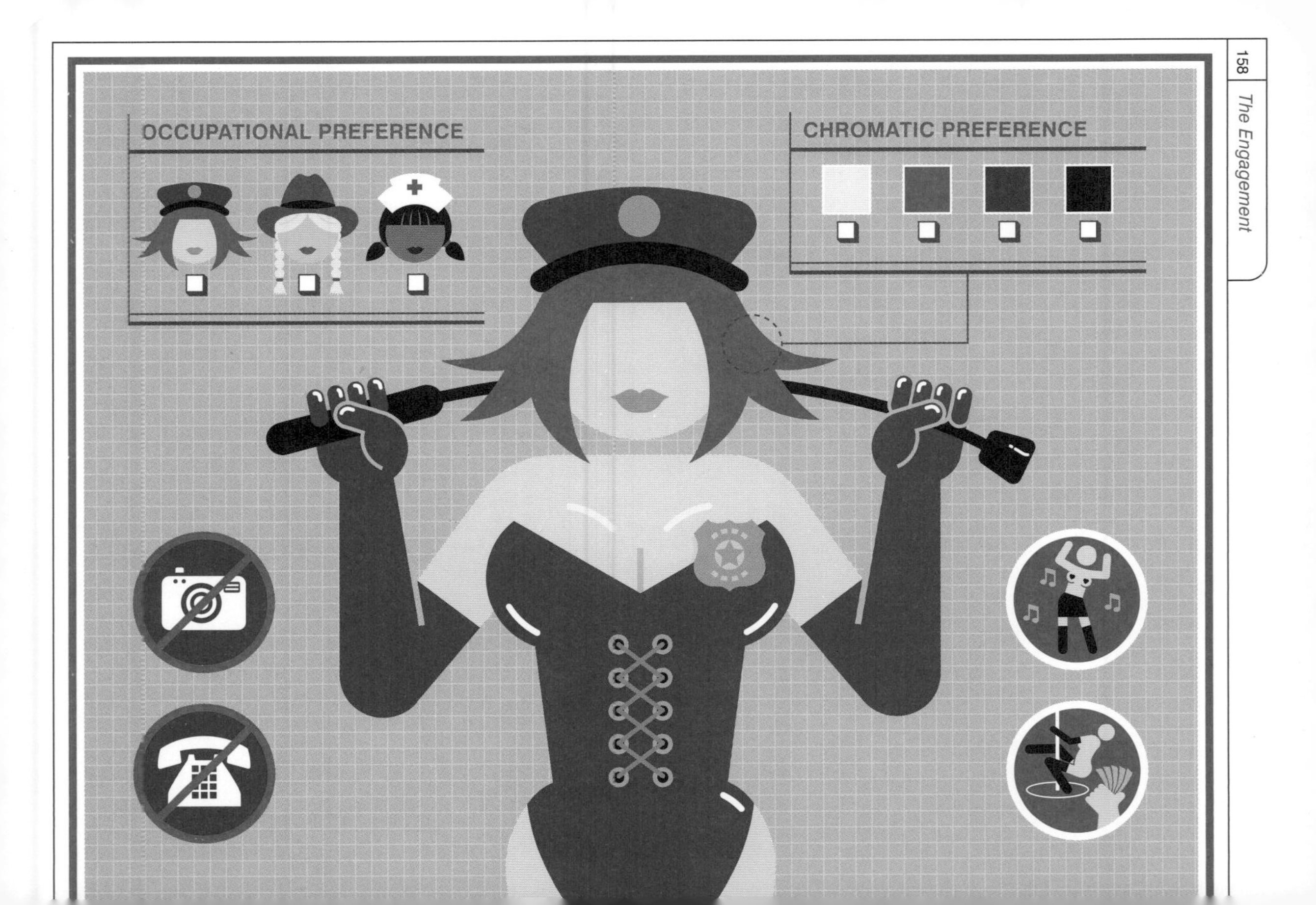
OCCUPATIONAL PREFERENCE
CHROMATIC PREFERENCE

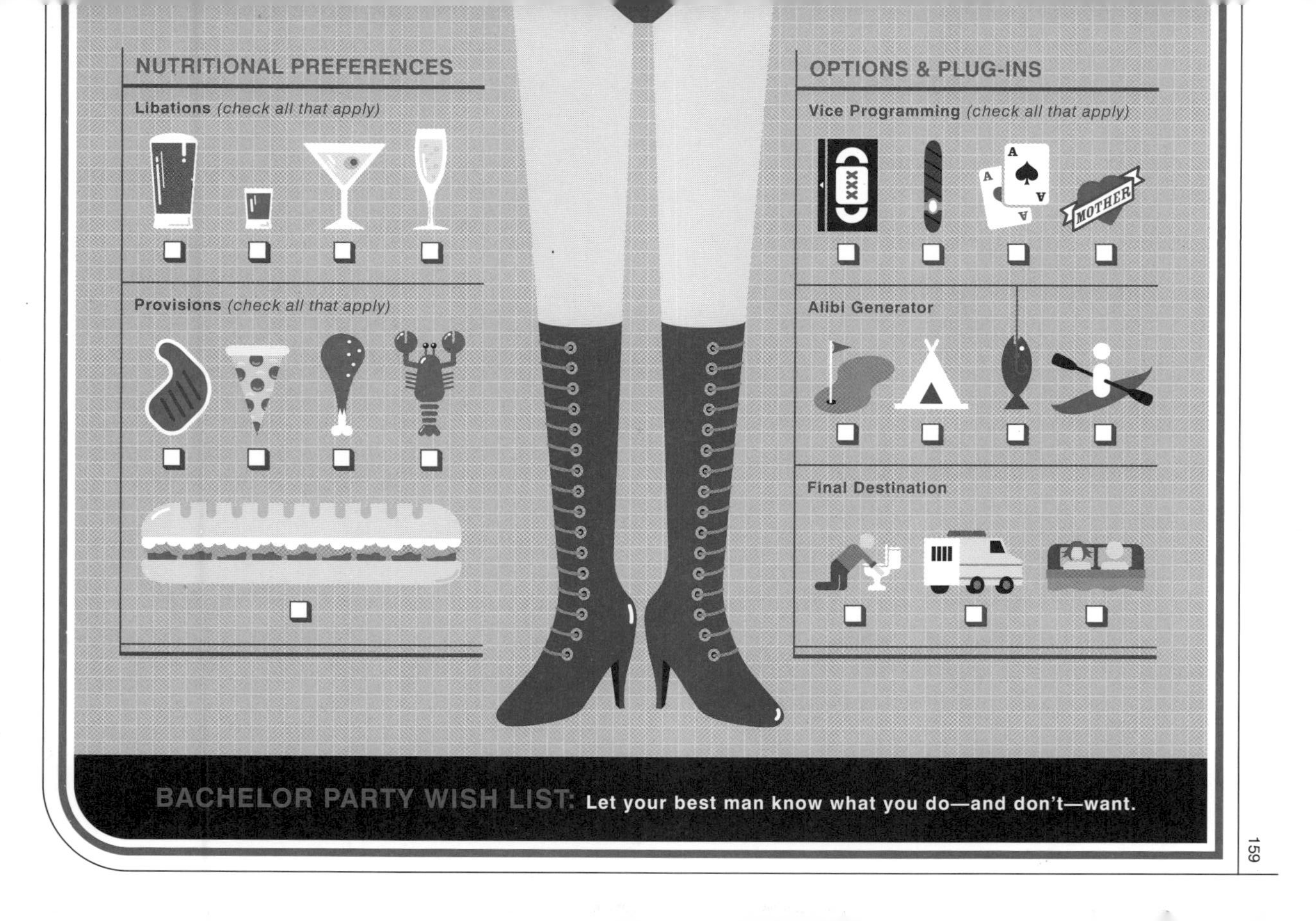
NUTRITIONAL PREFERENCES
Libations (check all that apply)
Provisions (check all that apply)
OPTIONS & PLUG-INS
Vice Programming (check all that apply)
XXX
A
MOTHER
Alibi Generator
Final Destination
BACHELOR PARTY WISH LIST: Let your best man know what you do—and don't—want.

Know What You Want

The bachelor party is a rare moment in the pre-wedding festivities when you can dictate exactly what should happen. Not your fiancée, not her mother, not the wedding planner—you. If there's anything in particular that you really, ***really*** want to do at your bachelor party—white-water rafting, helping out at a soup kitchen, getting spanked by a redhead—speak up, because your best man isn't a mind reader.

Know What You Don't Want

On the flipside, be sure to tell your best man what's absolutely off-limits. These might be things that your faith, tolerance, personal taste, pain threshold, or just plain good taste won't allow you to do. Again, your best man should respect your wishes; for your own good, however, we urge you not to settle for any old normal night out with the boys. Also, if you plan to make alcohol part of the festivities, you'll be surprised how quickly your morals can change.

Party for a Night or the Whole Weekend

In some circles it's popular to have an entire bachelor weekend as opposed to a one-night blowout. We're all for the idea if you have the stamina, but remember to consider the budgets of your groomsmen, who will already have other expenditures related to your wedding. Also, as with your wedding uniform, you may be able to benefit by making your travel plans in bulk.

Just Don't Party the Night Before the Wedding

Obvious, right? You don't want to be mumbling your vows through the fog of a hangover.

Legality Is Relative, Morality Is Not

Despite what your friends might tell you, this is not your last night navigating through lawless international waters, even if you are. While we cannot condone illegal activity, we're not about to ruin your good time if the only victim is you (and we're strictly talking nonviolent misdemeanors here). Anything that could compromise your marriage, on the other hand, should be out of the question, regardless how hard your friends push. In other words, if you think your behavior will get you in trouble with your fiancée, you're doing exactly the right thing. If you think it will bring the engagement to a quick and unceremonious halt, don't do it.

In Case of Extreme Emergency

Unless you and your fiancée are planning the simplest of weddings, you'll likely be presented with at least one occasion that will make you think your wedding plans, and hence your engagement, have derailed. Here are four of the most common situations you may encounter:

Your Fiancée Is Freaking Out

Planning a wedding is probably the most stressful event that you and your fiancée have ever tackled. Depending on your fiancée's demeanor (and/or the availability of supportive family members and/or competent wedding planners), it may simply be too much. If she seems to be cracking, remind her that everything is going well and that the wedding will be great. If her condition has progressed beyond such remedial reasoning, you might try mentioning the "E" word: elope. Generally, don't pull this card except in extreme circumstances—but if the wedding itself seems threatened by preparations, and the demands of family are overwhelming, eloping may be your ticket to happiness. Of course, this solution is not without pitfalls, such as alienating your family, wasting money, and missing the trappings of a planned wedding. However, if the choice is between a happy marriage and a soul-crushing wedding, always pick the marriage. Your family should understand, though perhaps not immediately.

Your Wedding Is Spiraling Out of Control

It may not be too late to change the size of the wedding. If the invitations haven't been mailed, cut down on your guest list and, if needed, seek out new venues. However, both of these tasks can in fact add more stress; if you're really having second thoughts, make the wedding smaller and pick a place easy to secure. Backyards can be ideal emergency backups—just make sure you know the person who owns the yard.

You've Been Bumped from Your Venue

This occurrence is not unheard of. You may also lose your venue to natural disasters, inclement weather, or even construction. Always remember the backyard bailout. Whenever you discover the news, immediately put your groomsmen to work moving tables and chairs, setting up tents, or doing whatever needs doing. It may not make for a picture-perfect wedding, but it could very well save your skin.

You No Longer Want to Marry Your Fiancée (or Vice Versa)

The fact is inescapable: People change their minds. If you and/or your fiancée are having second thoughts, we implore you to deal with the situation head-on. Talk through it, as painful as that may be. If your fiancée agrees, seek couples counseling. Postpone the wedding. Whatever you do, don't take your fiancée's behavior, or yours, as strict reality during engagement, because it's not normal life and it would be a shame to have a relationship dissolve under false pretenses.

On the other hand, if you're sure that things won't work out, or you believe things aren't going right on the grandest emotional scale, don't get married. It is practically, psychologically, and legally taxing to extract yourself from a relationship after you've signed that official certificate.

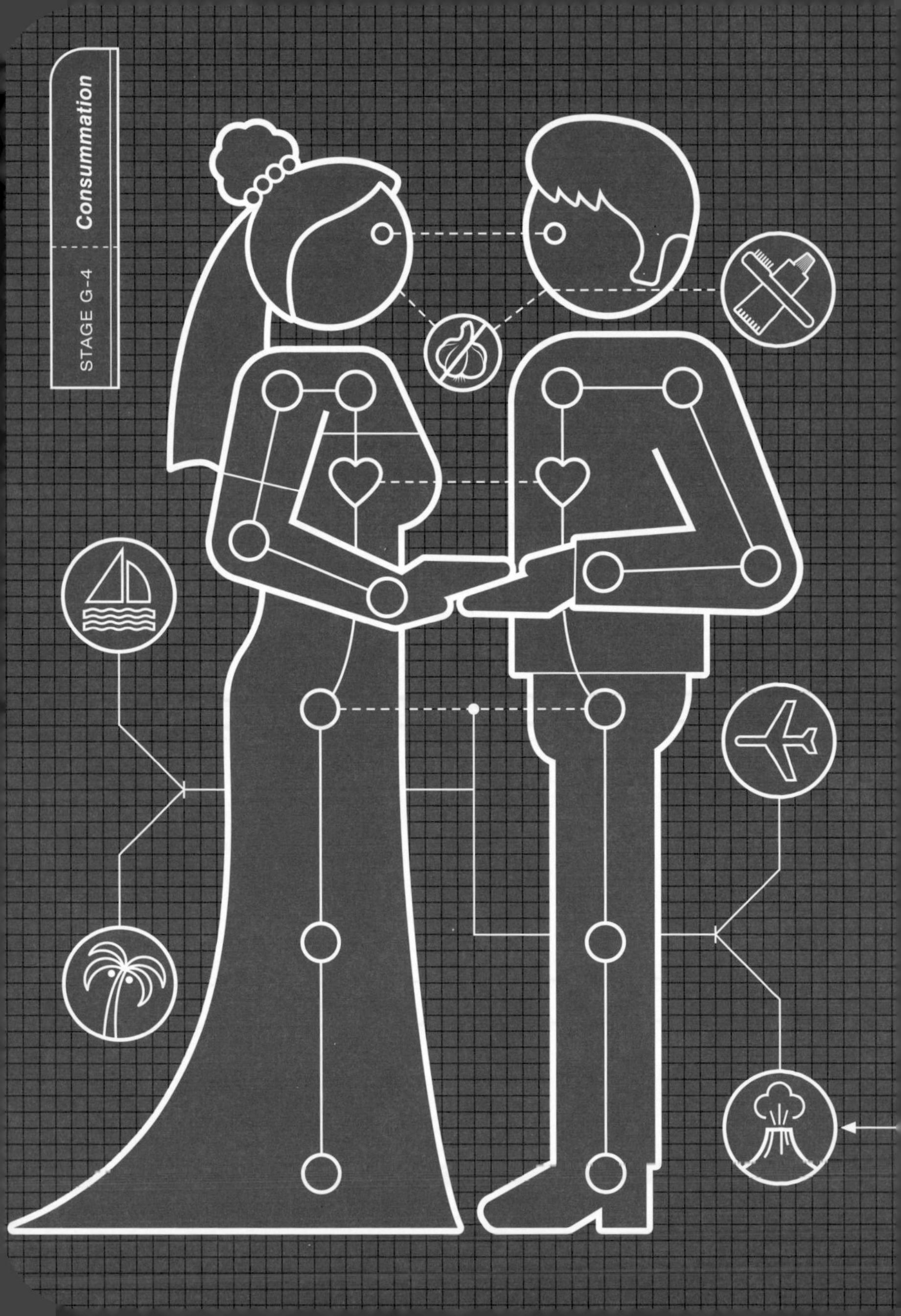
Consummation
STAGE G-4

[Chapter 4]

The Wedding

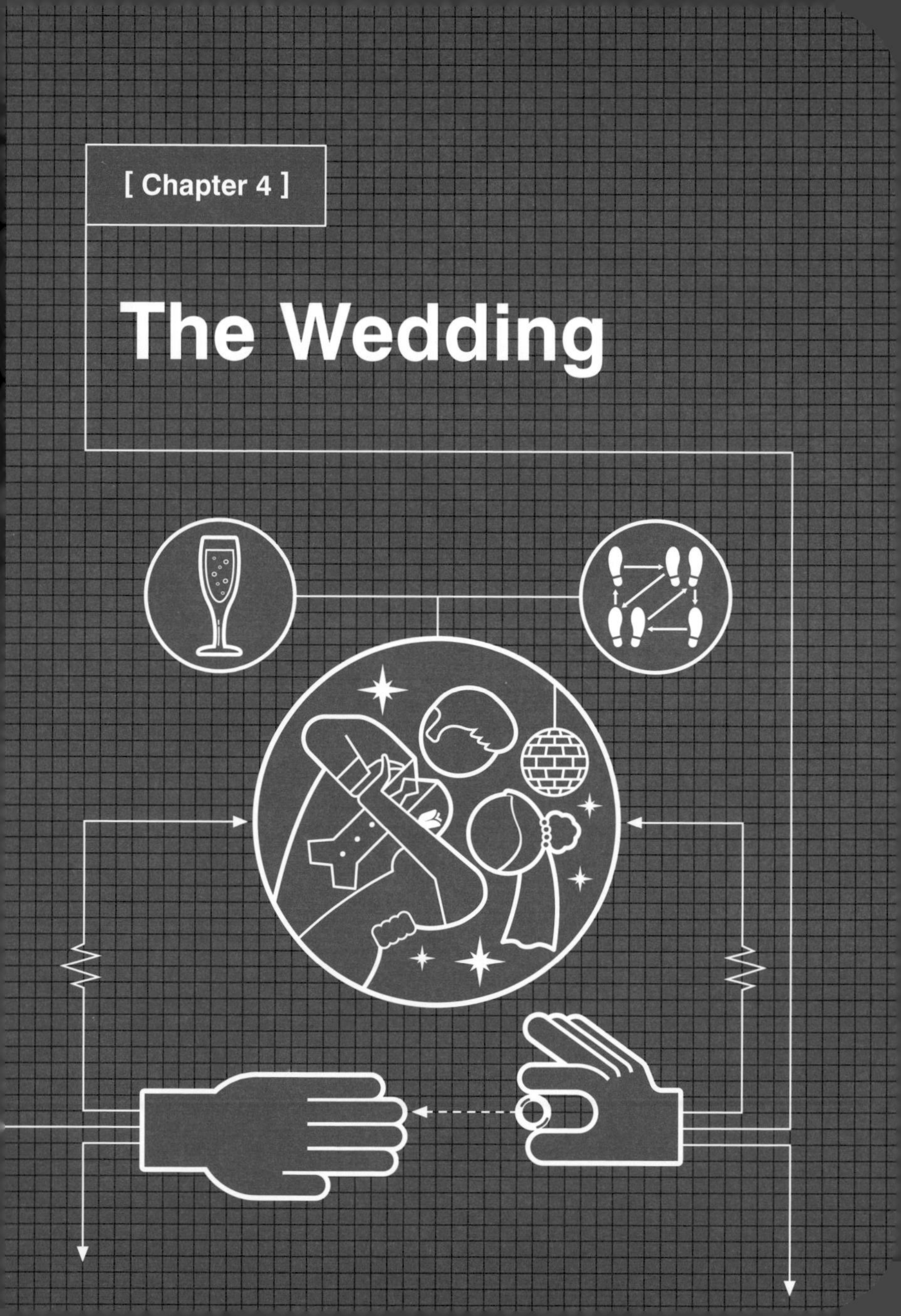

You may be surprised by the relative brevity of this chapter, but there's a reason it's so short: Like many life events, weddings are all about preparation. The ceremony itself is shorter than a sitcom. The reception might last four hours, or five if you serve lots of booze. The wedding-night consummation will last—well, not nearly as long as you'll tell your friends it did. So if you've prepared everything as described in Chapter 3, you can kick back on your big day, do what comes naturally, and have a great time.

Good Grooming

Like an actor, you will be required to fill a role on your wedding day and/or wedding weekend: yourself. Therefore, your preparation for being yourself should be precise yet familiar. You should follow your standard grooming habits where possible and change them where needed.

Hair: On their wedding day, many women will professionally style their hair so that every strand is perfectly coiffed. But men who visit their barber on said day will look like they just got a haircut. To avoid this unfortunate circumstance, visit a barber approximately one week before the big day. And, if possible, make sure this person is familiar with your hair and preferred style. Now is not the time to test drive a new look.

If you're bald, calculate the number of pre-wedding days necessary to achieve optimum stubble level and then proceed accordingly. Take your time with the razor to prevent tragic-looking wedding-day gouges.

It's best to trim facial hair about 3–5 days before the wedding, depending on how fast your mustache, beard, and/or sideburns grow. For other visible hairs—nose, ears, anywhere else—be sure to trim accordingly some 2–3 days before your wedding.

Nails: Your wife will be showing off her ring, and hence her nails, far more than you will. Yet your hands and fingers still play a large role in the wedding, so make sure your nails are looking sporty. You can get away with cutting them as much as a week in advance. If you "cut" your nails by gnawing on them, try as hard as you can to give it a rest in the weeks leading up to your wedding.

Body: Take a shower and clean yourself like you would when preparing for a date, if you can remember what that's like. Use soap, dumbass, but don't think you need to scrub yourself down until you're red.

Face: If you don't already own a good razor, now is a good time to spring for one. Shave like you normally would, and if you plan to wear any scented aftershave and/or cologne, do so to your fiancée's liking rather than your own. Chances are she'll prefer less aroma, no matter how manly, while you're saying your vows (anxious perspiration could trigger a stronger smell).

Nose: Blow it at the last possible, and sensible, occasion. If your fiancée is shorter than you, she may have a clear shot up your nostrils, so make sure they're as well groomed as the rest of you.

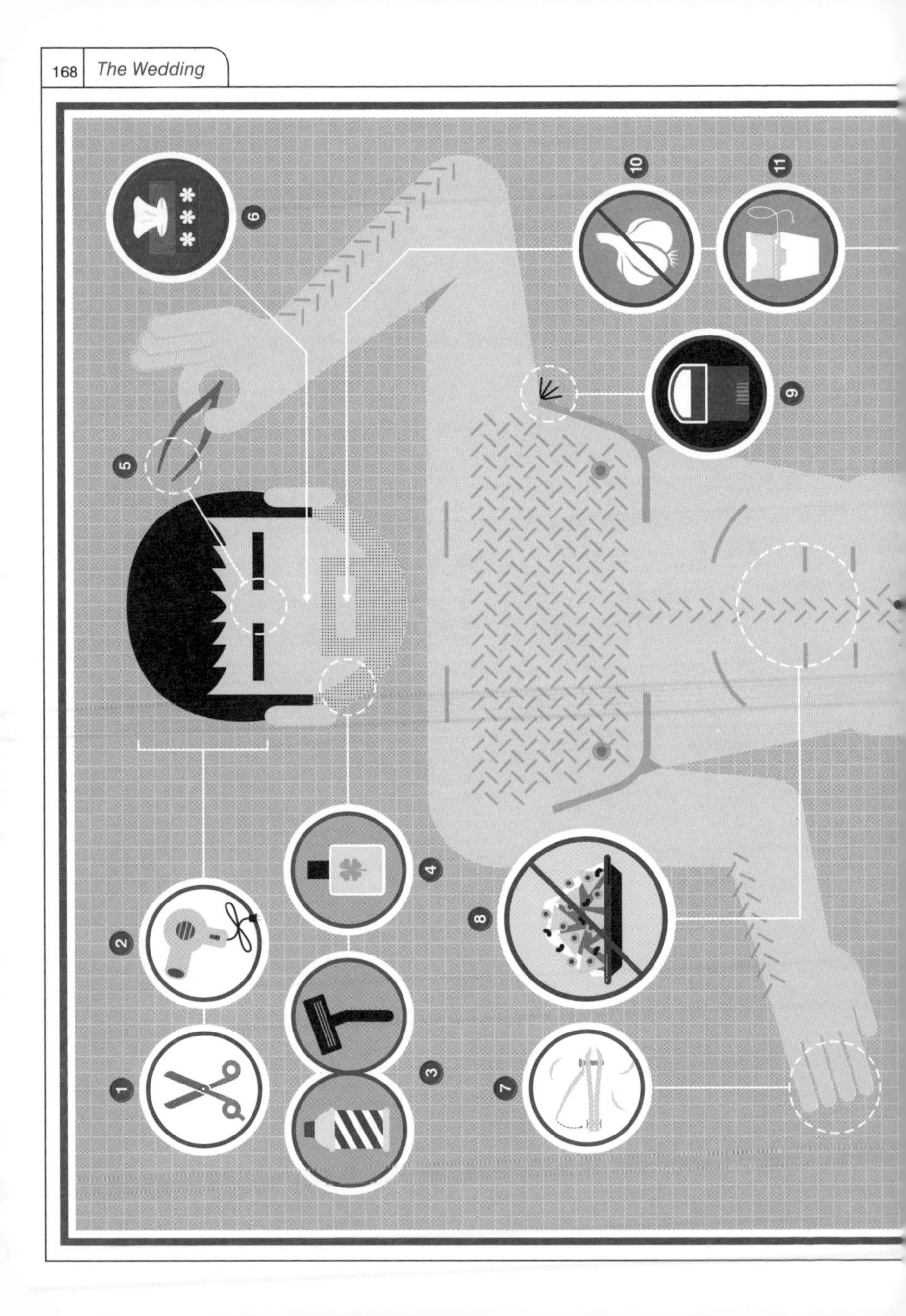
1
2
3
4
5
6
7
8
9
10
11

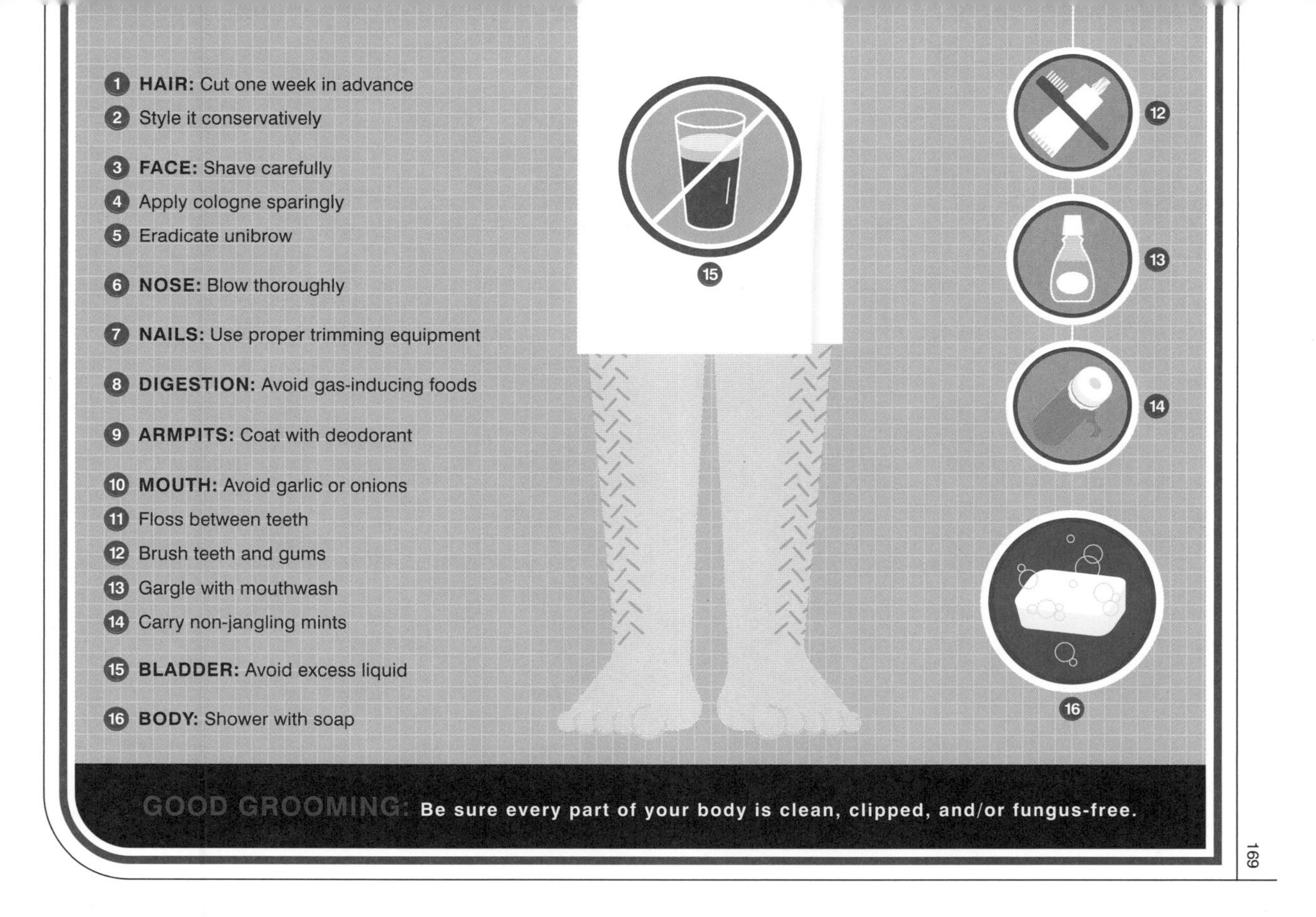

1 HAIR: Cut one week in advance
2 Style it conservatively
3 FACE: Shave carefully
4 Apply cologne sparingly
5 Eradicate unibrow
6 NOSE: Blow thoroughly
7 NAILS: Use proper trimming equipment
8 DIGESTION: Avoid gas-inducing foods
9 ARMPITS: Coat with deodorant
10 MOUTH: Avoid garlic or onions
11 Floss between teeth
12 Brush teeth and gums
13 Gargle with mouthwash
14 Carry non-jangling mints
15 BLADDER: Avoid excess liquid
16 BODY: Shower with soap
15
12
13
14
16
GOOD GROOMING: Be sure every part of your body is clean, clipped, and/or fungus-free.

Mouth: Avoid onions and garlic on your wedding day—you're about to spend hours talking to people, not to mention all the times you'll be kissing your bride. Brush your teeth as part of your overall get-ready routine. Also, consider mouthwash, and gargle it for the full thirty seconds. You should also stash a supply of mints in your pocket to get you through the day. But make sure they're removed from any plastic or metal containers so you don't make any jingly-jangly noises while walking down the aisle.

Armpits: Coat those bastards with deodorant/antiperspirant to your liking, keeping in mind that your nerves and formal dress might cause you to sweat more than normal. You should also consider wearing a light cotton undershirt if you don't already make a habit of it. You'll be walking and talking a lot, and the extra layer, while making you slightly hotter, will keep you from sweating all the way through your button-down shirt.

Bladder: You're going to be nervous, and you'll probably reach for anything that will quench your dry throat. But don't sip so frequently that you can't make it through the wedding ceremony (approximately thirty minutes for most, though some can run longer).

Digestion: Watch out for anything before the ceremony that could send your bowels into overdrive. Nobody likes a gassy groom.

Planning Your Weekend

These days, it's rare to find a wedding with events confined to a single evening; more and more weddings are becoming three-day weekend extravaganzas, consisting of a rehearsal on Friday, a ceremony and reception on Saturday, and sometimes even a brunch on Sunday morning. This expanded schedule will allow you time to catch up with friends, family, and everyone else attending the big event. Make a rough timetable of where you need to be and when you need to be there, share it with your groomsmen, and let them take over the rest. They'll likely be able to take the piss out of you if you show signs of a nervous breakdown. In fact . . .

Relax, Breathe, Go Fishing

Most rehearsals occur in the late afternoon or in the evening. If you've done your job well, every preparation will be made by now, and you'll have all day to sit around thinking, worrying, and stressing out. To prevent that from happening, ask your groomsmen to arrive as early in the day as possible. Spend the morning and early afternoon on a fishing boat, at a baseball game, or knocking down frames at the local bowling alley. Embrace mindless distractions. But watch your alcohol intake—you'll want absolute clarity at the rehearsal itself, which is probably just a few short hours away.

The Rehearsal

We begin this section with a very important point: This is your only shot to practice the wedding. You, your fiancée, and especially your groomsmen may be inclined to regale each other with inside jokes as you go through the motions of the ceremony—do so at your own peril. Come tomorrow morning, you want everyone walking down the aisle in the right order and arriving at their proper destinations. So keep the wisecracks to a minimum and pay attention.

If you have any special clothing or accessories (especially matching ties) to give your groomsmen, the rehearsal is the moment; waiting reduces the odds that one of your bozo buddies will lose or stain his tie. If the rehearsal will be followed by a particularly messy dinner (barbecue, spaghetti, and so on), perhaps wait until the morning of the wedding.

Finally, consult with your officiant about the marriage license and make sure all the paperwork is ready. It's the last thing you'll be thinking about on the day of your wedding.

Before You Go to Bed

We don't want to freak you out, but your life will totally change within the next twenty-four hours. It's enough to keep a guy awake at night. Indeed, if you are prone to anxiety, this will be like the night before your worst final exam—times one thousand. Fortunately, there are some remedies.

Talk to your fiancée. Don't turn out the light until you've told your fiancée how much she means to you. That will not only make you feel good and ease your mind a little, but ease her mind as well. And she'll appreciate you for it.

Talk to your boys. Yes, you've been doing a lot of this during the wedding weekend, and keep it going because that's why your groomsmen are there. Don't feel the need to talk about big life issues; it may even be better to talk about nothing at all.

Write a letter you may never deliver. Throughout your courtship and engagement, you've probably written a few letters to your fiancée—tonight, write one to your wife. If you want, you can give it to her the next day. Or don't give it to her at all. It's just an exercise to remind yourself why you're taking this monumental step. Channeling these good feelings onto paper may help put your mind at ease. Or the exercise may prove so tedious that you simply drift off to sleep.

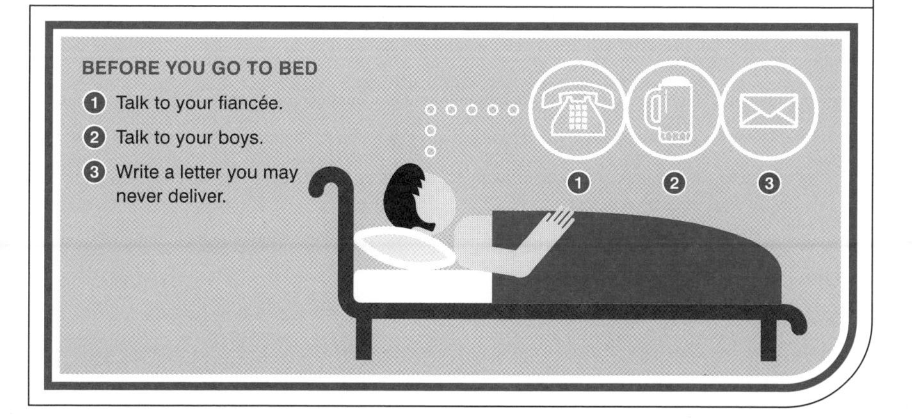

BEFORE YOU GO TO BED
1 Talk to your fiancée.
2 Talk to your boys.
3 Write a letter you may never deliver.
1
2
3

The Big Day

Here it is, the twelve to sixteen hours that you've been awaiting for the last, oh, say, twelve to sixteen months. Without knowing the specifics of your particular event, it's hard to coach you here, but most of you will be on the following timeline:

The Morning Of

Most people won't schedule anything too early on the wedding day, and for good reason: you need the time to rest up. Of course, set your alarm clock (or talk to your groomsmen) to ensure that you're ready when you need to be.

Trust in superstitions. Several superstitions surround weddings. Luckily, most of them pertain to the bride. The big one, of course, is that you're not supposed to see her before the ceremony. Whether or not you think it's silly, we recommend you give it a shot. Your fiancée is going to look gorgeous when she comes walking down that aisle, and the moment will be all the more special if it's the first time you've seen her all day.

Watch your diet. The foods you eat in the morning can hugely impact how the rest of your wedding day will go. Start off with a full and complete breakfast. Get your protein. But avoid problem foods—anything that will cause gas, indigestion, heartburn, bad breath, or other ailments. Pancakes and scrambled eggs are fine, but maybe pass on the onion-smothered breakfast burrito.

The Ceremony

You've been through the rehearsal. You know when to walk, where to stand, what to say. And you're probably well aware (though we'll say it again) that all eyes will be on you. So remember:

- Smile.
- Stand up straight.
- Hold your head up high.
- Keep your hands out of your pockets.
- Avoid shuffling and fidgeting.
- Make eye contact when being addressed.
- Use people's names when speaking to them.
- Don't swear. Especially if you're in a place of worship.
- Speak up. Make sure your voice carries when you say "I do."

Kissing the bride. It's a small point, granted, but remember that your wedding isn't a prime-time soap opera. Maybe you find it hard to contain your passion for your wife, but your guests (and your officiant) don't want to watch your tongue scrape the insides of her cheeks. Save the hot action for later.

The Reception

Here it is, the reason everyone showed up. Yes, some of the women came to have a good cry at the ceremony, but the reception is where the food, the booze, and the wedding band are hanging out, so it's where you'll find everyone else, too. It's your

RECEIVING LINE: To avoid repetition and enhance your receiving line

experience, here are several ways to welcome guests to your wedding.

moment to shine. Everyone will want to congratulate you, shake your hand, offer you advice, praise your performance, and get you a drink. It's quite a rush, so enjoy the adoration while it lasts.

⚠ ***Caution:*** *You'll be talking a lot, you'll be sweating a lot, and all your guests will be quick to fetch you a drink from the bar. Make sure you don't drink past your limit. An animated and exuberant groom can be charming, but nobody wants to see a drunk.*

Employ "handlers." As a celebrity, your time will be too valuable to squander on a single senile and/or drunken relative who wants to tell you every one of his thoughts on your wedding and how it relates to world politics. Unfortunately, you may not always be able to extricate yourself from these situations without offending someone. That's where your groomsmen come in. Your entourage has been at your side for the whole thing, through thick and thin, and now they need to rescue you from boring or otherwise hazardous conversations. Establish hand signals to clue in your groomsmen; "adjusting my necktie" may mean "find an excuse to get me away from this person." One or more groomsmen should come immediately to your rescue, explaining that your presence is required elsewhere.

The first dance. Perhaps the only thing more frightening than standing in front of God and all your family and friends to commit your vows of matrimony is doing the cha-cha in front of the same rapt audience. Yes, some of you will simply take your bride by the hand and lead her around the floor like Fred Astaire. But the rest of us will have to get by on a few simple tips.

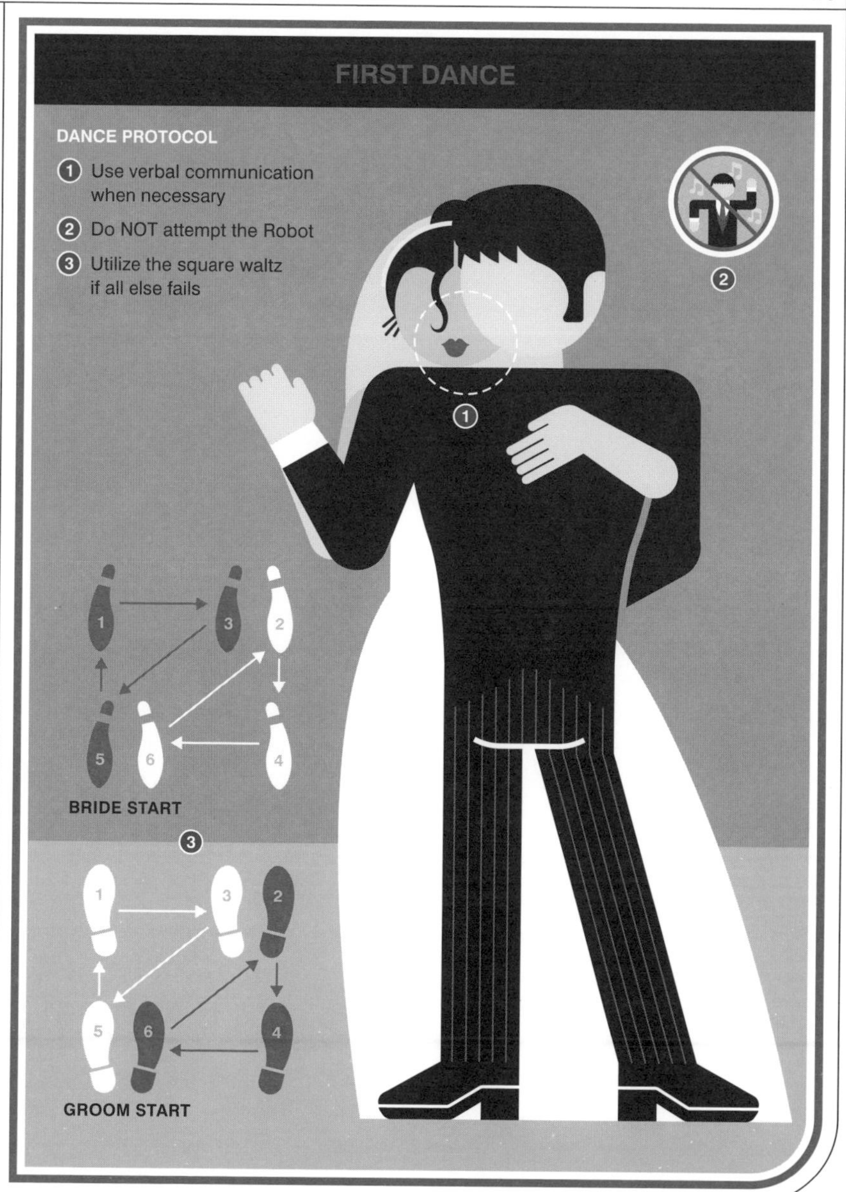
FIRST DANCE
DANCE PROTOCOL
1 Use verbal communication when necessary
2 Do NOT attempt the Robot
3 Utilize the square waltz if all else fails
2
1
1
3
2
5
6
4
BRIDE START
3
1
3
2
5
6
4
GROOM START

- **Apply the lessons you took.** If you read the last chapter and had the time to seek professional help, you'll be able to two-step, waltz, tango, do-si-do, or running man with the best of 'em. If not . . .

- **The square waltz.** By no means is that the official name of the dance. Rather, it's a standard dance to be used in case of emergency: step right, step back, step left, step forward. Repeat.

- **The Sway.** You'll want to avoid the junior-high slow dance, but there's nothing wrong with holding your bride close and slowly swaying. It requires just a quick shuffle of the feet back and forth, and it can possibly make you look like a hopeless romantic. But be warned that your fiancée may ask for more out of you than this lazy fallback.

- **Talk through it.** If she'll allow it, talk to your bride throughout the dance. Not only will it take your mind off how totally ridiculous you look, but it may also let her give you some tips as you're dancing.

- **Don't joke around.** Thinking of breaking out the Robot just to make light of how bad you are on the dance floor? Don't. You won't win any points with your bride if you revert to your sixth-grade habit of clowning to avoid embarrassment.

Stop to smell the overpriced flower arrangements. Weddings are similar to pregnancies: months of discomfort capped off by incredible pain followed by complete joy—all for the woman. The man just stands around confused, excited, and perturbed. In all the turmoil, it can be tough to keep sight of the importance of the occasion. You'll probably be tired, and you'll definitely be busy. If the post-ceremony euphoria starts to wear off too soon, don't be shy about giving yourself a quick break. Take a look around. Eat some appetizers. Lock yourself in the bathroom. Whatever works for you. Just be sure that you don't miss taking in the moment—and make sure your bride does the same. It would be a real shame if the two of you end the day without a couple hours of fun. And speaking of fun . . .

The Wedding Night

Whether your wedding turns out to be the party of the century or a nightmare gauntlet of in-law encounters and drunken toasts, the moment will arrive when it's time to bid adieu to your guests and retire to private quarters with the woman you love. This first intimate moment between spouses is much mythologized, and thanks to camcorders and the Internet it's also well documented by minor celebrities. Yet, after the nonstop excitement of the past 12–72 hours, this silent crescendo provides its own set of challenges.

Virgins

If you're among the rare few entering marriage without previous knowledge of carnal embrace, what you are about to experience is beyond the scope of this book. We suggest you pick up a companion handbook in preparation. However, we will offer one piece of

WEDDING NIGHT (VIRGINS)
(Fig. A)
12:02AM
(Fig. B)
12:06AM

advice: manage your expectations. It will be a magical moment, one that you'll never forget. But it will likely be just a moment, and it will most certainly get better with practice.

Everyone Else

Having already experienced that magic moment, and most likely with the woman who is now your wife, you may be overcome by another sensation: fatigue. You've spent a weekend entertaining guests. You've spent the past half-day or more dressed in a full suit and uncomfortable shoes while your wife has worn a dress tailored within a millimeter of her life. You've both been vowing, meeting, greeting, dancing, toasting, posing, and so much more. What you haven't been doing is eating, hydrating, and relaxing. None of that may matter as you carry your wife across the threshold and work on slipping the two of you into something more comfortable. But if the urge doesn't overcome you, don't feel bad—just come prepared.

Props

To keep your first night of marriage from feeling like too many of your subsequent nights, plant several props in the room before your arrival. Hopefully, you're still reasonably sober, so you and your fiancée might share a flute of champagne, or perhaps you'll just want to rehydrate with a few glasses of water. You should also plan ahead to have a groomsman and/or bridesmaid prepare

WEDDING NIGHT (EVERYONE ELSE)
1
2
3
4
5
① Chilled intoxicants ② Pre-packaged hydration ③ Nutritional sustenance
④ Zero-anniversary gift ⑤ High-definition camcorder (for posterity)

and deliver plates of food for you. You'll be surprised how little of this nourishment you even noticed at your reception, and you'll be ecstatic to have it.

Most important, be sure to have your Zero Anniversary Present (page 139) in the room. Even if your wife knows she has something coming, she'll appreciate the surprise, and her excitement may make her more inclined to consummate the marriage. Beyond these essentials, you should prepare additional surprises based on your relationship and your wife's personality. Lingerie is an old standby—though under most circumstances it should not be your wedding gift to her. Just make sure that it's something your wife will like (that is, if you saw it at your bachelor party, your wife probably won't like it . . . unless she was the one wearing it, in which case, hats off to you). Flowers can also contribute to the mood, and again you should pick them based on your wife's sensibilities—don't let an overzealous florist sell you her or his own version of romance. And, of course, be sure that the camcorder has a new tape, fresh batteries, and a sturdy tripod if there are plans to look back on the occasion with more than just fond memories.

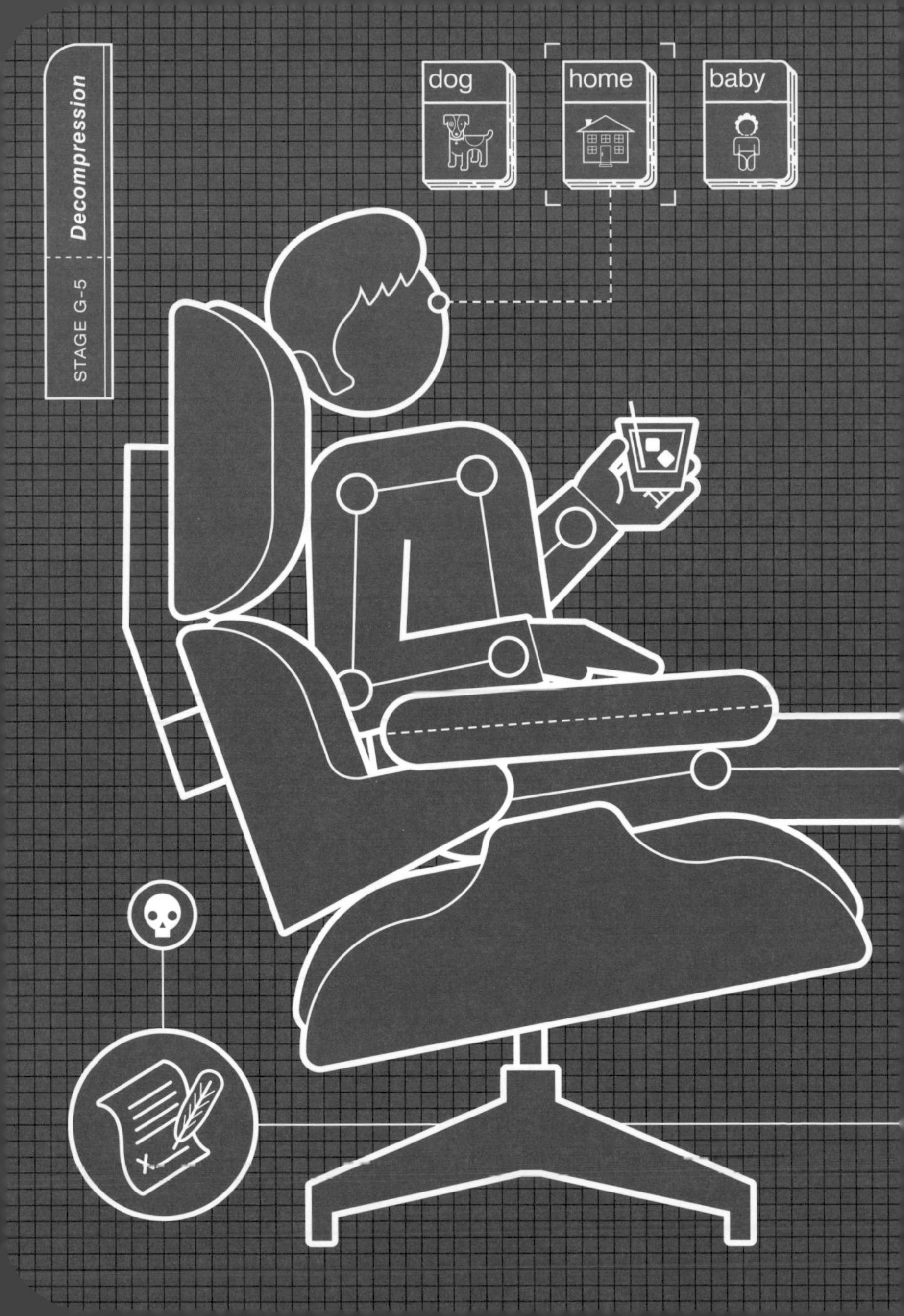
Decompression
STAGE G-5
dog
home
baby

[Chapter 5]

You're Married: Now What?

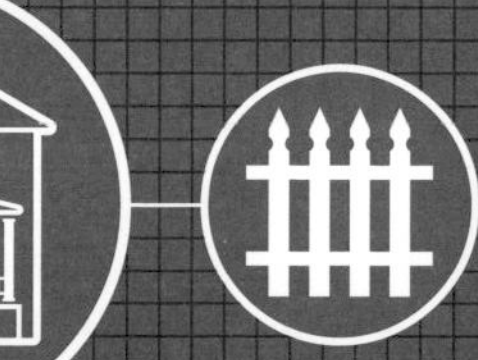

For you and your bride, getting married was a lot like the experience of famous children working in show business. For a brief, shining moment, you were a celebrity. Everybody wanted to shake your hand. People gave you gifts just because of who you were. Everywhere you turned, people were toasting you, photographing you, videotaping you.

Now, you're a mere mortal again. Child actors have traditionally turned to drugs, drink, crime, or Jesus to cushion their fall from grace. We recommend you take smaller, less drastic steps as you and your wife—yes, *your wife*—settle into your new lives.

Post-Wedding Housekeeping

So you're well rested and suntanned from the best honeymoon a couple could ask for—but believe it or not, the wedding still isn't over. You'll likely find yourself facing one or more of the following tasks.

- **Planning an After-Party:** Seriously. As if the rehearsal dinner, ceremony, and reception weren't enough, some couples will plan an additional "after-party" (usually in one of their hometowns) for those unable to attend the wedding. It's highly likely that your mother or mother-in-law will be in charge of planning this event, and you will have to do very little besides show up.

■ **Write Thank-You Notes:** Writing a note to every person who gave you a gift is a thoughtful gesture and—unless your wife is a saint—you will probably have to draft the notes to your friends and perhaps even your side of the family. Start practicing your cursive as soon as possible.

■ **Review Wedding Photographs and Video:** The photographer is likely to submit hundreds or even thousands of photographs for your review; depending on the deal, you may be asked to select personal favorites that will later be bound into an album. (Alternatively, you may receive only digital files or negatives of all the photographs, so you can create an album of your own.) Either way, it's a big job but likely one that you and your wife will enjoy doing together. As for the video, you may get just a final cut and that's that. But you may also want to be prepared to switch back into producer mode and tell the director which scenes to cut, which to expand, and so on.

■ **Pay Bills:** Few grooms escape a wedding clean and clear, so expect to pay some bills. They may be minor, or they may be stultifyingly huge. Whatever they are, work out a plan for paying them off without any defaults. The only thing worse than starting a wedding with an annulment is starting one on shaky financial ground.

■ **Settle Any Legal Disputes:** Likewise, if your wedding led to a brawl, stolen or damaged merchandise, public nudity and intoxication, a limo in a swamp, or all of the above, resolve your legal commitments

CONSTRUCTING A THANK-YOU NOTE

Dear _______________________,

(A) We were so happy you could attend our wedding!

(B) We were sorry you could not attend our wedding.
It was a wonderful day, and your presence was greatly missed.

(A) Thank you so much for our _____________________. It was exactly what we needed to make our ______________ complete.

(B) Thank you so much for your generous gift of $__________.
We put it to good use by purchasing a _____________________.

(A) We are looking forward to seeing you again—
perhaps at __________________________.

(B) We couldn't have asked for a more
[CREATIVE/ORIGINAL/GENEROUS] wedding present.

(A) All the best,

(B) All of our love,

____

⚠ ***CAUTION:*** *You will probably invite at least one guest who does not send a gift. If this happens, do the right thing and thank them for attending the wedding, anyway. Now that you're married, you need to get used to taking the high road.*

immediately. The only thing that should go on your record after your wedding is your new marital status.

Your New Wife

Just when you've finally gotten used to calling your girlfriend "my fiancée," you have to start calling her "my wife." This transition may be harder than you expect—you may even on occasion refer to your new bride as "this woman I just married" because somehow the words "my wife" are simply too difficult to say aloud. Over time, that will pass. And soon it will become second nature to call her "my wife"—not because that's who she is, but because that's who you want her to be. Here are some other ideas for kicking off your new life as a married couple.

Ease Back into Society

Just as returning veterans can find it difficult to reenter life outside the platoon, so too may you find going back to work and coming home to no engagement responsibilities a bit of an adjustment. "Where's the chaos?" you may ask. Well, it's gone, at least until you have children. This yearning for bedlam is why we suggested in Chapter 3 that, even if you and your wife can't spare the time or money for a full honeymoon, you should at least spend a relaxing post-wedding excursion before settling back

into home life. Honeymoons are rehab for weary wedding vets, and it behooves you to take your detox seriously.

Reclaim the Woman You Love

Remember that your wife is also going through a complicated transition—she has been drained of all the adrenaline, euphoria, and adoration that came from months of pre-wedding anticipation. In other words, her inner fiancée is slowly dying, and it will likely not be a death free from complications. Your best bet is to continue with the steps you learned for dealing with your fiancée while slowly making her realize that those days are over and she is now something altogether new: a wife. Force her to sleep in on the weekends. Buy her a box of chocolates or something she deprived herself of during the engagement. Take her out on a date. Do whatever you think will help her feel special in a different way than being a fiancée made her feel.

Go Back to Being Equals (Yeah, Right)

The wedding was her thing, but the marriage belongs to both of you. Right? Yes, and a peaceful resolution to all wars around the globe is just around the corner. It's true that individual personalities can lead to any number of marriage dynamics, but expect that most of these dynamics will end up with you being wrong and your wife being right.

If you think this notion is straight out of television sitcoms, try being married for a few months and see how things go. Perhaps you'll get lucky and have a relationship in which small disagreements are uncommon or, better yet, when they do happen you're as likely to come out on top as your wife. The reality is that women, regardless of language or culture, have an uncanny ability to turn conversations in their favor. Even if they're dead wrong, even if a blind man could draw the flaws in their arguments, there are still 2-to-1 odds that she will get her way over you.

Rather than fighting against this inevitability, we recommend that you embrace it. If your wife wants to carry on in her role as the responsible person who gets to have a say in everything, from your utility bills to the grocery shopping to the color of the rec-room carpet, let her do so. And then buy yourself a comfortable chair.

Keep It Real

Don't expect to get comfortable in that chair too soon. After an eventful wedding, it's easy to let the malaise set in before you even realize it. To avoid the anxiety of thinking you made a mistake only a few months into the wedding, keep acting like you're not yet married. Consider employing any of the suggestions from "Keep the Romance Alive" (pages 144–145) or feel free to improvise your own.

General Housekeeping

In addition to the psychological challenges of adjusting to married life, several practical steps will help you make your marriage legitimate.

Playing house. If you don't already live together, then, first of all, heaven help you, and second, remember to abide by this very simple rule: Let your wife do the interior decorating, and focus your efforts on moving boxes. Some of you may take issue with the wife controlling the house to such an extent. If you do indeed have the appropriate background (read: you're an interior designer or architect), then by all means have some say in the appearance of your new home. If not, don't fight a losing battle. Your wife is going to get all the credit (or blame) for your house regardless of how it looks, so you might as well let her earn it.

Joint accounts. If you haven't done so already, consider getting a checking and/or savings account in both your names. In fact, if your wife plans to change her last name, you will have to get a joint checking account because you will likely receive a few wedding gifts in the form of personal checks addressed to both of you. If you're close enough to tie the knot and sleep in the same bed every night, we hope you're close enough to share a bank account.

Review your tax status. Getting married does crazy things to your status with the IRS—some good, some bad. Don't hesitate to talk to a C.P.A. who specializes in income tax so that you're sure to get the most out of your new status.

Update insurance policies and/or wills. Yep, they're not automatically updated just because you're married. If there's anything you want to make sure your wife receives with the least bit of governmental/court interference, make sure to note it in a will and on your life insurance policy. If things have already gone sour and you want to make sure your wife doesn't pull an Anna Nicole Smith (God rest her soul), you should likewise check with your attorney or draft a will specifying that your last wishes don't include a drawn-out court proceeding.

Think about the future. Yes, this one's very ambiguous. We just put it here to freak you out.

Happily Ever After

Now it's time to say good-bye. We hope you enjoyed your wedding. Your new wife is a being wholly unique from your fiancée or your girlfriend, and she has unique traits you'll soon discover—but that's a subject for a different book. Suffice to say that you should keep your new wife happy, just as she should keep you happy. In today's era of quickie divorces and common-law marriages, that can be a tall order. But in planning and enduring your wedding, you've experienced something pretty enormous, and you're a better man for it.

One last suggestion: You should probably start thinking about that first anniversary gift because she'll know if you've waited until the last minute.

ANNIVERSARY GIFTS

YEAR	TRADITIONAL	MODERN
1	Paper	Clocks
2	Cotton	China
3	Leather	Crystal
4	Fruit or Flowers	Appliances
5	Wood	Silverware
6	Candy or Iron	Wood
7	Wool or Copper	Desk Set
8	Bronze or Pottery	Linens or Lace
9	Pottery and Willow	Leather
10	Tin or Aluminum	Jewelry
15	Crystal	Watches
20	China	Platinum
25	Silver	Silver
30	Pearl	Diamond
35	Coral	Jade
40	Ruby	Ruby
45	Sapphire	Sapphire
50	Gold	Gold
60	Diamond	Diamond

[Appendix]

Contact Info

Use these documents to record contact information in your wedding. When possible, be sure to obtain

GROOM'S PARENTS

MR. ○ DR. ○ ______ ○ & MRS. ○ DR. ○ ______ ○

Address (Number and Street) | **City**

State/Province | **Country** | **Zip/Postal Code**

TEL ☐☐☐ – ☐☐☐ – ☐☐☐☐ ○ HOME ○ WORK ○ CELL ○ FAX

TEL ☐☐☐ – ☐☐☐ – ☐☐☐☐ ○ HOME ○ WORK ○ CELL ○ FAX

TEL ☐☐☐ – ☐☐☐ – ☐☐☐☐ ○ HOME ○ WORK ○ CELL ○ FAX

TEL ☐☐☐ – ☐☐☐ – ☐☐☐☐ ○ HOME ○ WORK ○ CELL ○ FAX

TEL ☐☐☐ – ☐☐☐ – ☐☐☐☐ ○ HOME ○ WORK ○ CELL ○ FAX

E-mail (Father) | **E-mail (Mother)**

for the various people and places that will play an important role
a mobile telephone number so you can make contact at any time.

BRIDE'S PARENTS

MR. DR. ____ & MRS. DR. ____

Address (Number and Street) | City

State/Province | Country | Zip/Postal Code

TEL ___-___-____ HOME WORK CELL FAX

TEL ___-___-____ HOME WORK CELL FAX

TEL ___-___-____ HOME WORK CELL FAX

TEL ___-___-____ HOME WORK CELL FAX

TEL ___-___-____ HOME WORK CELL FAX

E-mail (Father) | E-mail (Mother)

Contact Info

Use these documents to record contact information
in your wedding. When possible, be sure to obtain

BEST MAN

MR. DR. ____

TEL [ ][ ][ ] – [ ][ ][ ] – [ ][ ][ ][ ] HOME WORK CELL FAX

TEL [ ][ ][ ] – [ ][ ][ ] – [ ][ ][ ][ ] HOME WORK CELL FAX

E-mail

Instant Messager

MAID/MATRON OF HONOR

MRS. DR. ____

TEL [ ][ ][ ] – [ ][ ][ ] – [ ][ ][ ][ ] HOME WORK CELL FAX

TEL [ ][ ][ ] – [ ][ ][ ] – [ ][ ][ ][ ] HOME WORK CELL FAX

E-mail

Instant Messager

for the various people and places that will play an important role
a mobile telephone number so you can make contact at any time.

OFFICIANT

Title | Name

Congregation

Address (Number and Street) | City

State/Province | Country | Zip/Postal Code

TEL ☐☐☐–☐☐☐–☐☐☐☐ ◯ HOME ◯ WORK ◯ CELL ◯ FAX

WEDDING PLANNER

MR. ◯ MRS. ◯

TEL ☐☐☐–☐☐☐–☐☐☐☐ ◯ HOME ◯ WORK ◯ CELL ◯ FAX

TEL ☐☐☐–☐☐☐–☐☐☐☐ ◯ HOME ◯ WORK ◯ CELL ◯ FAX

Contact Info

Use these documents to record contact information in your wedding. When possible, be sure to obtain

MUSIC/ENTERTAINMENT

BAND ◯ DJ ◯ SINGER ◯

Web Site | **E-mail**

TEL ☐☐☐–☐☐☐–☐☐☐☐ ◯ **HOME** ◯ **WORK** ◯ **CELL** ◯ **FAX**

PHOTOGRAPHER

Name/Company | **Web Site**

TEL ☐☐☐–☐☐☐–☐☐☐☐ ◯ **HOME** ◯ **WORK** ◯ **CELL** ◯ **FAX**

VIDEOGRAPHER

Name/Company | **Web Site**

TEL ☐☐☐–☐☐☐–☐☐☐☐ ◯ **HOME** ◯ **WORK** ◯ **CELL** ◯ **FAX**

for the various people and places that will play an important role
a mobile telephone number so you can make contact at any time.

CATERER

Company | Contact

Address (Number and Street) | City

State/Province | Country | Zip/Postal Code

TEL ☐☐☐–☐☐☐–☐☐☐☐ ◯ HOME ◯ WORK ◯ CELL ◯ FAX

FLORIST

Company | Contact

Web Site

Address (Number and Street) | City

State/Province | Country | Zip/Postal Code

TEL ☐☐☐–☐☐☐–☐☐☐☐ ◯ HOME ◯ WORK ◯ CELL ◯ FAX

Index

G

H

I

J

K

L

M

T

U

V

W

Z

About the Author

SHANDON FOWLER was the intrepid copilot of a "traditional Southern wedding" in his wife's hometown of Beaufort, South Carolina. The ceremony took place in front of 500 friends and family members, with a bride-to-groom invitee ratio of 8 to 1. The reception was held under a giant oak tree in his mother-in-law's yard (an idyllic setting and a big money saver). It was either a picture-perfect wedding or an experience so traumatic that it will take years to recover, depending on whom and when you ask. Shandon resides in Brooklyn, New York, with his wife, Sydney, and their son, Spence.

About the Illustrators

PAUL KEPPLE and **JUDE BUFFUM** are better known as the Philadelphia-based studio **HEADCASE DESIGN**. Their work has been featured in many design and illustration publications, such as *AIGA 365* and *50 Books/50 Covers, American Illustration*, *Communication Arts*, and *Print*. Paul worked at Running Press Book Publishers for several years before opening Headcase in 1998. Both graduated from the Tyler School of Art, where they now teach. When Jude married his art school sweetheart, Amy, a suitable human to take up the task of ring bearer could not be located. Fortunately their Boston Terrier, Huxley, was persuaded to bear the mantle, after a few laps of Yuengling Lager settled his nerves.

At Last! A Comprehensive Guide to Good Grooming

Gone are the days when you could sit back and let your fiancée plan the entire wedding. Today's grooms have countless tasks to perform, from hiring the entertainment and planning the rehearsal dinner to buying the wedding bands and comforting hysterical family members.

Fortunately, *The Groom's Instruction Manual* is here to answer all of your most challenging questions: How do I handle feuding relatives? What should I look for in a good wedding photographer? Why does my fiancée seem stressed out all the time? Whatever your concerns, you'll find the answers here—courtesy of author and veteran groom Shandon Fowler.

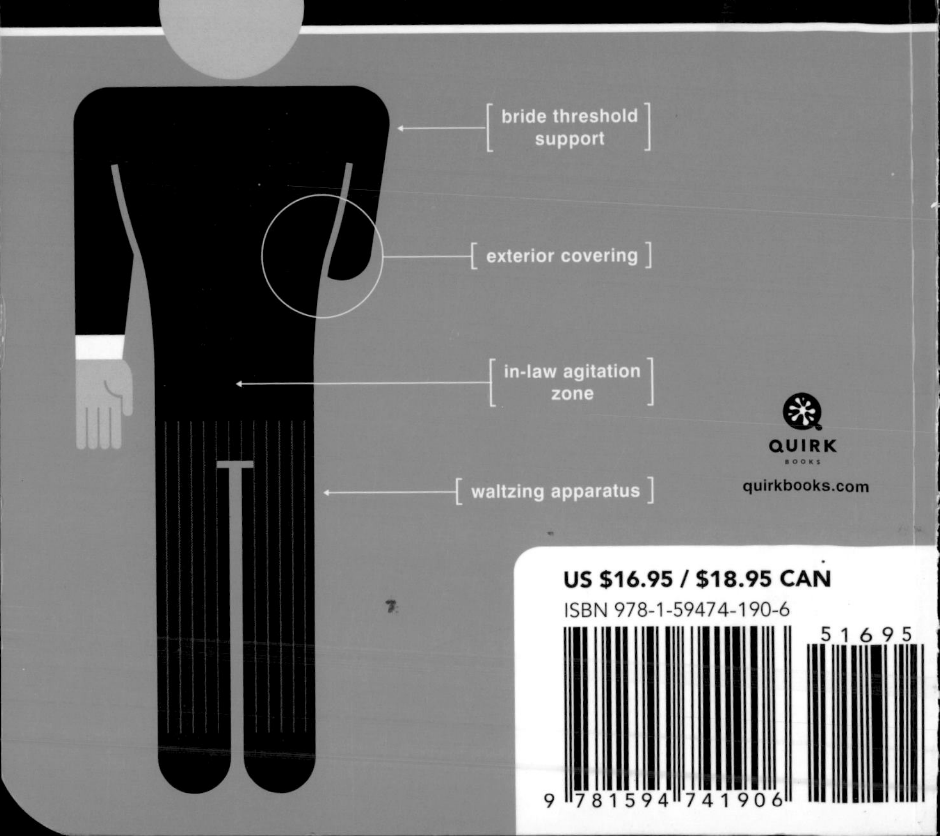

US $16.95 / $18.95 CAN

ISBN 978-1-59474-190-6

51695

9 781594 741906